Of War and Love

DOROTHEE SÖLLE

Of War and Love

Translated from the German by
Rita and Robert Kimber

ORBIS BOOKS
Maryknoll, New York 10545

The Catholic Foreign Mission Society of America (Maryknoll) recruits and trains people for overseas missionary service. Through Orbis Books Maryknoll aims to foster the international dialogue that is essential to mission. The books published, however, reflect the opinions of their authors and are not meant to represent the official position of the society.

First published as *Im Hause des Menschenfressers: Texte zum Frieden,* copyright © 1981 by Rowohlt Taschenbuch Verlag; GmbH, Reinbek bei Hamburg, West Germany. A selection was made from the German original for the English translation. Also, additional poems have been included from *fliegen lernen* and *spiel doch von brot und rosen.*

"Against the Death Machine" appeared in 1980 under a different title in *Assoziationen,* vol. 3, ed. W. Jens, copyright © Radium Verlag, Stuttgart.

"A story from the talmud and questions for us" is from F. Duve, H. Böll, K. Staeck, eds., *Kämpfen für die Sanfte Republik* (Reinbek: rororo aktuell, 1980).

The poems "The kingdom of god or the great consensus," "Chile summer '78," and "Girl from chile" are taken from the volume *fliegen lernen,* copyright © Wolfgang Fietkau Verlag, Berlin, 1979.

The other poems in this volume are taken from *spiel doch von brot und rosen,* copyright © Wolfgang Fietkau Verlag, Berlin, 1981.

The text "To crucify" first appeared in *Politisches Nachtgebet,* vol. 2, ed. D. Sölle and F. Steffensky, copyright © Kreuz Verlag, Stuttgart.

English translation copyright © 1983 Orbis Books, Maryknoll, NY 10545
All rights reserved
Manufactured in the United States of America

Bible quotations are from the Jerusalem Bible

Manuscript Editor: William E. Jerman

Library of Congress Cataloging in Publication Data

Sölle, Dorothee.
  Of war and love.

  Translation of: Selections from Im Hause des Menschenfressers, with additional poems and stories included.
    1. Peace—Poetry. 2. Peace—Addresses, essays, lectures. I. Title.
PT2681.O33I413 1983   831'.914   83-8252
ISBN 0-88344-350-3 (pbk.)

Second Printing, May 1984

For Fulbert

toper and waterer of wine
first and last reader
father confessor in resistance

who knows the night
and lights the candles
to read the book

who protects me
from others and myself
and gives up on nobody

except himself sometimes

compañero

Contents

Alphabetical List of Poetry Titles

Foreword

The major task that good persons should set themselves is to teach others to say no.

— *Pierre J. Proudhon, 1858*

The country of which I am a citizen—Germany—did not say no in 1914 or 1933 or 1939. In response to the question "Do you want total war?," thousands upon thousands of my compatriots screamed yes.

Not quite forty years later a new question was posed: "Do you want a total arms buildup?" This question is never put so openly, of course. Even though the NATO leaders in Brussels have more power over the life of every school child in my country than does any official I could vote for, they do not have to seek or obtain any democratic consensus. The total arms buildup—which is to say, the nuclear arms buildup—simply goes on; the public is not informed, the public is not educated, the public does not vote on the issue. The ideology of "security" has made all those things superfluous. I do not call this state of affairs "defense preparedness." I call it "militarism," a time-honored German tradition dressed up in new technology.

The word "peace," all by itself, appears less and less often in the speeches of leading politicians. And when it does appear, the feeling is that it should not be used all alone and "unprotected." It has to go hand in hand with "security." Once there has been enough loud and explicit military talk about security, then there is nothing threatening about adding "and peace" at the end. First things first, and the first thing we need is absolute security.

But as every marriage counselor knows, a desire for absolute security produces just the opposite; it produces increased insecurity and self-destruction. When the desire for security becomes neurotic, it no longer protects us but rather leads to our destruction. And our collective need for security revealed itself as neurotic in December 1979—when NATO decided to station nuclear missiles in Europe, and we agreed. The superpowers' capacity for mutual assured destruction is indeed mad. But insight alone cannot dispel collective neuroses any more than it can individual neuroses. Demons have to be exorcised.

It is no mere wordplay to speak of "SSecurity." The two S's in this spelling, alluding to the infamous Nazi *SS,* call attention to the genocide that is being practiced today in El Salvador, in South Africa, and in many other places. We are supporting that practice in the name of a worldwide economic dictatorship that we help maintain and that can survive only under military protection. "SSecurity."

How can we teach our fellow citizens to say no instead of "Yes, sir! Right away, sir!"? How can we teach ourselves to say no loud enough that we will be heard? How can we speak patiently and objectively enough for those who want to know the truth and do not just swallow every fairy tale that Washington puts out? How can we be militant and informed enough to influence those who think everything that comes out of Stockholm or London is nothing but communist propaganda? How can we bring strength and encouragement to those who have known the truth for so long that they have become cynical and bitter?

The texts against militarism that I am presenting here are meant to be aids to articulation. They are texts in the cause of peace, even though some of them have to do with torture, violations of human rights, and the perpetuation of hunger in the interest of profit. The two parts of the book complement each other, just as do economic planning à la Milton Friedman and security planning à la Alexander Haig ("There are more important things than peace").

The provenance of these texts and the dialect they speak is that of the Judeo-Christian tradition. What I want to stress, though, is not so much the Judeo-Christian love of peace, which is a sufficiently publicized element in that tradition, but rather the human capacity to *make* peace, an element that—in German Protestantism at any rate—has received much less attention. To be a Christian in the context of the militarism that holds sway over us demands that we do more than hum some apolitical Christmas carol. We have to be a little more explicit than that.

By "explicit" I mean that we have to become as militant, as nonviolent, and as illegal in our actions as Jesus and his friends were. As I write this, friends of mine—among them Dan and Phil Berrigan—are standing trial in Norristown, Pennsylvania. The group calls itself the "Plowshares Eight," taking its name from Isaiah 2:4: "They shall beat their swords into plowshares." On September 9, 1980, these eight men and women entered a General Electric plant in King of Prussia, Pennsylvania, where re-entry nose cones for nuclear missiles are built. With hammers they destroyed two Mark 12A nose cones, and they poured human blood on secret blueprints.

When I say we have to be "more explicit," I mean that it is high time that Germans too adopt the methods of civil disobedience that have been developed in other countries. This book is intended as a call to resistance so that we can learn deliberate violation of the rules, nonviolent illegality, and civil disobedience together. It is possible to violate laws and regulations governing property without committing violence against human beings. Our imaginations in this area are underdeveloped. If we want to take part in liberation movements, then the militarism that dominates us is our main enemy.

Nonviolent actions run the risk of being ineffective. Perhaps we just do not have enough experience with disobedience, resistance, and the violation of rules. Petitions, letters to government officials, leaflets, and demonstrations alone are not enough to combat the arrogance of power that manifests itself most clearly in militarism. The democratic character of nonviolent illegality has to be made visible. We, too, have to start plucking a few ears of corn on the Sabbath.

Jesus' disciples broke a religious law when they did that. They acted illegally; they were present where they had no business being; they touched what they had no business touching; they violated a rule that was regarded as sacred in their society. The most sacred thing in our country is private ownership of the means of production. If this private property serves the cause of death, it is more sacred still, more deserving of protection, subject to more powerful taboos. Any violation of these taboos is decried as "violence," even though a violation of this kind has as little to do with violence as a motorcyclist's helmet does with a weapon. The excessive preoccupation with violence in our country is symptomatic in itself. All I have to do anywhere is raise the subject of hunger, torture, the resurrection of Christ, or the death wish in our culture, and it will not be long before someone asks me what I think about violence.

Is it violence if the disciples pluck corn? Is it violence if the Plowshares Eight make two atomic warheads unusable? Is it violence if a blade of grass forces its way up through the presumably impenetrable asphalt? Is the action of water on stone violence? Is it violence when Hansel and Gretel do in the wicked witch?

We have a great deal to learn, and civil disobedience puts its faith in the human capacity to learn. Human beings can and do undergo conversion. That is one of the messages of Christianity that no one can forget with impunity. The blind learn to see; the lame learn to walk; and those who have always been ruled and regulated and ordered around learn to resist. We should not let the mass media, which seem to be all-powerful but which really play into the hands of the state machinery, determine how we conceive of education, how consciousness is shaped, or how peace can be made. The growth of the peace movement in West Germany is a sign of our strength.

And, dear non-Christian readers, prayer does help. Do not be narrow-minded. What I am talking about has almost nothing to do with organized religion. It has to do with us ourselves and with what we want, what we must not give up in exchange for the drivel that is always being handed us. Of course prayer helps. And knowing that we are one with the power that helps the blade of grass break through the asphalt. Wishing helps, and dreaming, and talking together, and having a vision, and communicating that vision in our actions.

PART ONE

To Rebel Means
to Organize Resistance

"We shall be free only when we join forces with life against production for death and the ongoing preparation for murder. We shall not become free by retiring into the private sphere and saying 'Count me out.' Nor shall we become free by conforming to a society that holds its generals and millionaires in particularly high regard.

"We shall become free when we learn to work for peace actively, deliberately, militantly."

D. S.

1

In the house of the man-eating ogre

Born in the era of gas
I found myself later in the house of the ogre
his wife comely and plump
took me in looked after me
gave me plenty to eat
and hid me from him
when he came home

Life isn't so bad
in the house of the ogre
during the day he goes about the land
stationing missiles
ruining highways
and training young men
for deployment at home or abroad
for the distant enemy
the ogre displays
his famous first strike
to those in his own land
who still talk back
even after heavy doses of radiation
he has dogs and gas of course
I myself am free to come and go as I please during the day
in the house of the ogre
I joke with his wife and don't fret about anything

Only in the evening when he comes home
and sniffs around and looks for me
do I tremble with fear
in my little bombproof box
then I dream
about dismembered bodies
and about starving yellowish children
then I hate my father and mother
for bringing me into this world
at this time
and in this country

Someday
it's never been any different
the ogre will eat us
that's the way it's always been
up to now

Blessed Are the Peacemakers

Sermon delivered in the Lübeck Cathedral,
September 6, 1980

Brothers and Sisters,

We have just said in unison: "Blessed are the peaceloving."* I'd like to suggest two other translations of this verse. The one, which is very close to the original, is: "Blessed are the peacemakers; they shall be called the sons of God." The other casts a little more light on the somewhat vague word "blessed": "All who create peace may rejoice; they will be God's children."

I should like to tell you about a theology student and motorcycle-enthusiast I met a little while ago, a student of the new breed, one without any background in the humanities but with plenty of practical passion, one who does not care for baroque music but who "rocks against the Right." This student, Rüdiger, told me about his experiences in the *Bundeswehr* (the West German army). I tried later to write down in his own words what he had said. This is what he told me:

> You either go along or you've had it. They stick you in the barracks, and suddenly your private space is cut down to practically nothing. I had to fight to get a room to myself at home. It took me a long time. Now you can't hang up anything; no place for it. You live for the next weekend when you can see your girlfriend. Maybe it would be better to be in

*Translators' note: This is a literal translation of Luther's *Selig sind die Friedfertigen*. The version of this passage (Matt. 5:9) most familiar in English is the King James reading: "Blessed are the peacemakers; for they shall be called the children of God." In the Jerusalem Bible, the line reads: "Happy the peacemakers; they shall be called sons of God."

that box all the time instead of half there and half at home. But that's not the only thing that gets to you. They tell you about ABC warfare—atomic, bacteriological, chemical—how it works, and all that stuff, and they try to tell you it's not so bad. You just duck behind the closest hill, if there's one around; then you find out where the atomic explosion was and then you report it. Everybody knows that's baloney, but they all go along with it. The only way you can stand it is to take drugs and drink. The *Bundeswehr* doesn't understand that. Either you adjust, let them do anything they want with you, stop thinking—offensive wars for NATO, sure! why not? that's all old hat—either you go along with it, or you're finished. For later, too. When you get a job you live the same way; you let them do what they want with you as long as the pay is good, or you don't go along with it. You start putting things together, see what I mean? And it takes you beyond just facts. You're in it right up to your neck. You're so mad you could scream. You're beginning to understand something you'll never forget the rest of your life. You start thinking!

Rüdiger wound up in the *Bundeswehr* the way thousands of others do. "There was no choice, not with my background," he said. But he began to ask questions, applied for a discharge on grounds of conscience, was refused, and applied again. Now he is studying theology.

What fascinated me about his story was the point where he began to rebel. The space he had struggled for at home was suddenly taken away. "The same thing could happen if you were doing alternative service," I pointed out to him.

He said: "But that's completely different. There you know what you're doing it *for.*" To rebel, to defend yourself, to know what it is you're living for—those are among the most important learning experiences we can have. If Rüdiger had not rebelled, he probably would have gone the normal route like everyone else. He would be "dead" now, as he puts it, which is to say he would be doing his job somewhere in an office or a plant. He still wonders why most of his fellow soldiers did not join him when he began to rebel, why they were so afraid of their own feelings, why they preferred to play dead. Rüdiger cannot understand that. And the more I think about it, the less I understand it.

I think that the biblical verse *Selig sind die Friedfertigen* as we know it in Luther's translation contains a hidden danger. It encourages us to be passive, peaceful bystanders like that famous tailor from Saxony who put up over the door of his shop a rhyme dedicated to his sovereign, the prince of Saxony: *Unter deinen Flügeln kann ich ruhig bügeln* ("Under your protective wing I live in peace and do my ironing"). If that is the meaning of "blessed are the peaceloving"—and among most German Protestants it is the accepted interpretation—then it is a distortion of what Jesus meant. This translation is not right, and we will have to learn a different translation, one that is true to the original, a translation that emphasizes the active process of "peacemaking," of "working for peace." And that means rebelling.

How do we become "makers" of peace? I think one aspect of rebelling has to do with the self that we no longer hide and keep in anonymity. When Rüdiger could not stand life in the barracks anymore, everyone knew who he was. When he stopped holding his feelings in check, he became visible. He became a "nut," a "kook."

Anyone who questions authority and rebels against it contributes a portion of his or her own life to, let us say, an institution that is in no way prepared for that contribution and that is not designed to make allowance for rebellion. To give of yourself means to make yourself known. The Gospels say of Jesus that he cast out demons because they knew him. He had become known. He intervened in the sicknesses of others, even though their illnesses were their own business; and he rebelled against the rule of the demons who were in charge.

Institutionalized domination is a demonic business; it has gone beyond our control and likes to pretend to be almighty Fate in person. A prohibition on questioning and rebelling is a means of exercising power. You are not supposed to ask what kind of war is going on, whether it is being fought to defend a neighboring country that has been attacked or to win control of that most vital of all commodities: oil. That is no concern of yours. Whether A, B, or C weapons will be used is none of your business. But to rebel means to make yourself visible so that others know it is *you,* that

7

Two or three things I know about michael

Michael tells how in the army
he refused to touch a rifle
and when they yelled idiot at him
he studied agriculture to be a farmer
you want my boot up your ass
he found the courage to yell back across the drill field
I'm a conscientious objector
then they all laughed michael says with his straight face

Then he was sitting alone facing his locker
he had to wait and got scared
sounds funny michael says with his eyes wide open
but I read the bible
and all of a sudden I wasn't scared anymore

Taken before an officer he was told
after two hours
why should the *bundeswehr* waste its time running
someone like you into the ground
and all of a sudden
most faces looked crooked to me
and most eyes closed

kook who is always spouting off at the mouth, that guy or that gal who is never satisfied. Rebelling, not letting them do what they will with you, means running those risks.

Another component of rebellion is "mixing it up" in the literal as well as the figurative sense, the creation of disorder, the confusion of jurisdictions and competences. Jesus created a jumble wherever he went. Ties of blood and family were immaterial to him; whoever did the will of God was his brother, his sister, his mother. In other words, he mixes private and public matters together. He does not abide by the rules that permit intimacy with only a few persons and require remoteness and indifference toward the many. He tosses everything into one pot and stirs it all up together. Religion and faith suddenly have a bearing on politics. The mentally ill suddenly find themselves in contact with all kinds of people and not, as before, just with psychiatrists and other specialists. Democracy has to do, then, with involvement, with "mixing it up," and not with defining areas of competence or with intimidation by experts.

If we want to learn how to initiate change and become peacemakers ourselves, then we have to learn to give of ourselves and mix things up. We have to learn to give ourselves up, to make ourselves known, and to get rid of the divisions in our world that jam everything into a predefined order. For it is these divisions that have led us to where we are now—on the verge of a third world war. Our time—that is, the period after the NATO decision of December 1979—has often been compared with 1914. International tensions have increased to such a degree that it would take only one small miscalculation on the part of a single leading politician or one small computer error to bring about world catastrophe.

I think we shall all have to change if we want to do something about this. I think that we shall all have to change. I think the question of whether the individual or the structure of society has to be changed first is a relatively stupid question.

Rebels try to change the world around them, and at the same time they will see that they are changing themselves as well. But only through rebellion is change possible. Any other form of learning is comparable to—and no more useful than—filling a cup with coffee. True, the cup may be full for the time being, but it is still the same cup. If learning amounts to no more than this, then we have not changed ourselves, and we are powerless to change anything else. As long as I continue to be treated like an empty cup in school, at work, in church, or in political life, as long as I let myself be treated that way, I cannot change, because I have not questioned and rebelled. Even God cannot change anything with commandments or promises. Healing, making whole, becoming new cannot be accomplished by infusion but only by personal involvement.

In Christianity, the technical term for this involvement, for God's involvement in the world, is incarnation—the word become flesh. God, in the form of Jesus Christ, involved himself in the economy, in politics, in the way we treat the mentally ill, in challenging militarism. God wanted to change something; he needed to then, and he still needs to.

Loving does not mean giving someone a present, something valuable that the other can make no use of. That would be a one-sided relationship in which one person does the pouring and the other person is the cup into which something is poured. Loving means to make someone else's capacities productive. God does not treat us as if we were empty cups, even though theologians sometimes talk as if God did. "The peacemakers shall be called the children of God." Ordinarily we become sons or daughters simply by being born and not because of our actions; and as a rule we therefore have no say about whose child we shall be. But in this case, in God's case, things are different. Those who make peace will be God's children. Here we do have a say; we are involved. We—as creatures who can assume personal responsibility—have an active role here. Those who act as God does—which is to say, those who make peace—will be called God's children. That is how I understand this Beatitude. God set out to create something together with us, something new that we call peace, freedom, justice. God began work on this kingdom of God; without our cooperation God will not get any further with it. But because God took an active role, we can, too. We can carry on God's work.

To clarify this point I should like to express it in negative terms: if we do not take part in this work, and as long as we do not, we are without God. I am not talking about anything special or religious here. I am talking about our normal everyday lives in which we just continue to plod along doing our jobs without hope, without

10

strength, without involvement. As Rüdiger put it, "You've had it." Or, as the slogan says, "If you don't fight back you're on the wrong track." Anyone who is not questioning has stopped learning, and anyone who is not learning is dead. "For why will ye die?" Ezekiel asked. "Cast away from you all your transgressions, whereby ye have transgressed; and make you a new heart and a new spirit: for why will ye die, O house of Israel?" This all becomes clear when we translate it into concrete terms. In our world, the greatest transgression against those who want justice and peace is the militarism that we tolerate and against which we do not rebel.

I am not thinking in utopian terms here but in realistic ones. I am talking about our closest neighbor, a small nation on our own border. I am talking about the Dutch, who rebel in a way we do not and for whom one world war is apparently enough whereas we do not seem to have learned our lesson from two. The Dutch have assumed an active role in the cause of peace. The placards they carried in their demonstrations before the NATO decision read "Disarm—Yes! Modernize—No!"

The Dutch parliament voted against the stationing of medium-range missiles on Dutch soil. It was like a touch of rainbow in a dark sky. We should be grateful for their action, grateful that some people in Europe realize what is important, know what is in store for us, and know what to do to prevent it. How much personal involvement it must have taken, how many young people must have experienced what Rüdiger did. How many discussions, congresses, radio programs, articles, demonstrations, worship services, and prayers must have prepared the way for that vote. How many contradictions to the claims of the experts that more missiles mean more security when in reality they mean greater danger. As if it were not enough that we can kill every single Russian eleven times over, as if that were not security enough. The Dutch have rebelled, just as they did a few years ago when they refused to drink coffee from Angola, coffee that tasted of blood, they said. They made that clear to every last citizen, and they are doing the same thing now. It makes me frantic to think the Dutch can accomplish what my country with its much bloodier history, with its dreadful history, cannot accomplish, that Germans continue to see this decision for a continuing arms buildup as a bagatelle and do not understand at all what a massive step has been

11

taken toward the mobilization and militarization of our entire society.

Unless we take responsibility for the here and now, the past is of no use to us. We have learned nothing from it. Our dead have died in vain if we do not rebel now. Against whom are we arming ourselves? Against the Russians? Are the Russians really our enemies—or is Washington our enemy? Is it not the arms race itself that is destroying us? Are we not arming ourselves against the starving populations of the Third World? To whom are we denying our help? Whom are we subjecting to the market laws of world trade and to the death by starvation that is incorporated into those laws?

In a leaflet put out by the American peace movement I found the sentence: "The bombs are falling *now*." That sentence taught me a lot. I had thought before that the arms buildup was a kind of preparation for something that might happen later and perhaps will never happen. But if we consider what it means to say "the bombs are falling *now*," then we realize that the arms race that consumes our money, our taxes, our intelligence, and our efforts is destroying our own country, too, and that it will not allow the Third World to achieve peace or justice or to feed its hungry people. Half of the scientists in the entire world today work directly or indirectly for the arms industry. Half of all our scientific minds are at work to increase overkill, to devise better bombs and better plans for mass murder. Americans call this combination of economic interests, scientific research, and military power the "military-industrial complex." If I wanted to describe it in biblical language, I would call it the beast, the huge beast that rose up out of the sea, the beast with seven heads: more energy, more progress, more overkill, more profit, a larger world market, more torture, a higher standard of living. I am afraid of this beast with its seven heads. Because I am afraid, I have begun to rebel. I am trying to organize resistance. That is why I am here. Subjugation kills. It kills every one of you. Your soul can die from this subjugation, from just going along with it, from not objecting, from choosing—once more—not to know.

We are already waging war against true life. We are waging war against the natural world that we exploit. We are waging war against our own need to live a simpler life, a need that we have to

Praise for my fatherland

Birds are nesting in parts of my country
that have long been deserted
this very summer a village was built in my country
with a fountain and a church square
before the bulldozers came
so the excavating could proceed undisturbed
some young men in my country feed hospital patients
and clean up old people rather than learn to shoot
there are women in my country who
without a thought for their own smooth skin
work to keep the skin of others
free of napalm cancer and military decorations

Of all these
birds villages young men doing alternative service and
women committed to resistance
there are not enough in my country
to prevent a third world war
of all these
there are not enough

repress or postpone. We live in a state of cold war between the rich and the poor, and the poor are perishing in it. The bombs are falling now.

The people we exploit and abandon are starving to death *now*. They are falling on what in naiver times was called "the field of honor."

Rebelling means organizing resistance. Since December 1979, when NATO decided for a new arms buildup, our society has undergone a militarization that can be documented with innumerable small examples. We are supposed to be taught to accept a third world war as a possibility. This is supposed to become a familiar idea for us. Until now, the *Bundeswehr* has been kept in the background and has not occupied a particularly prominent position in our society. But now it is being pushed into the limelight.

Let me cite just a few other examples of this militarization in West Germany. The question of "women in the military" has suddenly been given a major play in the mass media. A cleverly timed and placed interview set the ball rolling. The issue is discussed. Participants in these discussions come up with some feminist arguments saying, for instance, that women would be more equal if they too were trained in combat skills.

Another example: the swearing in of army recruits has been made a public event, and great media coverage is expended on the grandiose ceremonies. Something important is going on here, something we should be proud of, and it has to be shown in the proper light.

Another example: one of the most important needs of military personages has been rediscovered—namely, the need to wear medals. Until now this need was not felt to be so important, but it has been dug up again, a minor symbolic gesture that is profoundly revealing of the militarization taking place in West Germany.

Still another example: conscientious objectors are being discriminated against. The state reserves to itself the right to pass judgment on their consciences. The peace movement has tried to explain—in accordance with the Protestant interpretation of what conscience is—that conscience cannot be measured by any external yardstick, but these attempts have been quashed. Military authorities continue to examine and pass judgment on individual consciences.

When I ask myself what in our country is going right, what is justified in human terms, what we can be proud of, one of the first things I think of is alternative service, those thousands of young men doing dirty, menial jobs. Without them, any number of social and charitable institutions could not function at all. They are the true "heroes of the nation." They are displaying more courage, strength, and staying power than most. But in our society, they are the last to receive recognition for these qualities.

The growing militarism in our country reduces even further the chances for the survival of populations in the Third World. At the same time that it threatens the future of our children, it destroys life in the present. It deprives us of the capacity to become sons and daughters of God, to become peacemakers. If we make militarism our God for whom no sacrifice is too great, if security is the golden calf that we worship and give up all else for, then we are turning away from the living God, and we fear and love militarism. But if we do that, we are deceiving ourselves and destroying our own lives. We cannot just go along. We cannot just quietly put up with this. We cannot say "Amen" to it. We cannot just "go on ironing in peace." Not with impunity.

To question and rebel means to organize resistance. What we need now and what we will need in the coming years is a broad, comprehensive resistance movement against militarism, a movement that includes members of every political grouping from the center to the left.

We have to take up the cause of peace, take sides with life, interfere nonviolently and illegally. I think we can learn the most for our purposes from the liberation struggles in the Third World. I have been given a leaflet from the resistance movement in Chile, a leaflet that can be distributed there only at the risk of one's life. These Chileans are reflecting on their situation, on what it means to live under a dictatorship and what is happening to them as a result. I think we can adopt a great deal of what they say for our own situation, for they say: "Rebel! Don't cooperate with death! Choose life!" They also say, "Don't let them steal away your soul! Amen!"

15

Blessed are the peacemakers

*Prayer of intercession after the above sermon in the
Lübeck cathedral, September 6, 1980*

Jesus our brother
you break the rifle in two
and make your followers
fearless and militant
   those who rule over us say catch up
   and mean buildup
   they say defense
   and mean intervention and first strike
   they say peace
   and mean oil
Jesus let us become like you and not put up with the lie
we will not put up with militarism
not over us not next to us not in us

Lord have mercy . . .

Jesus our brother
you disrupt weapons deals
you butted in
you organized resistance
   we have hidden from the misery of the poor
   we live in an opulent palace bristling with weapons
   we build up our defenses and let others starve
Jesus let us become like you and not put up with their dying
we will not serve militarism
not with words not with money not with our life's time

Lord have mercy . . .

Jesus our brother
you bring the death industry to a halt
you drive the desire for absolute security out of our hearts
you free us to defend ourselves
    the generals in our country want to wear medals again
    it will cost only a hundred and fifty thousand marks
    you were betrayed for only thirty pieces of silver
Jesus teach us to understand what life is
that those who do not fight back are on the wrong track
let us become your brothers and sisters who make peace

Lord have mercy . . .

Your voice, comrade

In the middle of talking
with a comrade engaged in the same struggle
I suddenly know beyond the shadow of a doubt
we have nothing to say to each other

Once the situation has been discussed
the possibilities assessed
the work assigned
we have nothing to say to each other

Our hands only touched in passing
your voice comrade never changed
do you have only one
I forgot to look into your eyes
I don't know what color they are

I'm dismayed
but I can't communicate
even that

What's the matter with us

Are the struggle and our concern
and the defeat and the defeat after that
not enough to draw us together

Has the coldness of the world
penetrated us to the bone

What are we waiting for
the kingdom of god can come only
if it's already here

And what does the ogre look like?

In a photograph taken at the *rheinmetall* factory
I count five animate beings and seven artillery shells
the animate beings are dressed in suits white shirts and ties
which leads me to think that they are men
their hair ranges from thick to thinning to sparse
which leads me to think that they are in their mid-thirties
    to mid-fifties

All but one are exposing their upper front teeth
which leads me to think that they have just made a profitable deal
all of them hold on to the weapons they have produced
with one hand or both self-confidently proud or buddylike
which leads me to think that they love weapons
their self-confidently proud or buddylike stances lead me to
    think in addition

that they would like to have colossal pricks
all the representatives of the weapons firm shown here
(with the exception of the unsmiling one whose half-open
    mouth gives him an idiotic look)
strike me as dynamically precise and decisive
which leads me to think that they will determine my german fate
as has happened twice before in this century
unless we strip them of power

Against the Death Machine

With Him, Like Him

> *That evening, after sunset, they brought to him all who were
> sick and those who were possessed by devils. The whole town
> came crowding around the door, and he cured many who
> were suffering from diseases of one kind or another; he also
> cast out many devils, but he would not allow them to speak,
> because they knew who he was [Mark 1:32–34].*

"He also cast out many devils, but he would not allow them to
speak, because they knew who he was."

I do not want to continue reading this text as a report about
something that happened a long time ago. I want to translate it into
the fluid, equivocal reality in which we live.

There are demons on the loose among us, horrible creatures with
immense powers, bloodthirsty creatures addicted to death. They
are called Belial and Samiel. They live in dark deserts, far from
cultivated lands. But they are as restless and mobile as top
managers. They invade villages and cities and take possession of
people, both individually and in groups. They subjugate entire
countries, forcing obedience from them. The people in whom these
demons have taken up residence scream and moan with pain, but
they cannot free themselves. Do they really want to? The ill and the
possessed are brought to Jesus; at least their relatives want the
sufferers to be healed.

This is a horror trip. The demons drink our blood, with the
approval of our parliament. They call for "more." Stronger,
bigger, louder, better, they cry. Nobody wants a horror trip, but
who resists a "good trip"? To be better than everyone else, to be
the greatest, to leave others in the dust—who does not want that?
So we go on our "trip." We consume more energy; we refuse to

accept a speed limit on the *Autobahn*; we build nuclear power plants. A big trip holds out the promise of great happiness—that is, a high standard of living. Granted, we have to run a few risks to attain this high goal, a little war of conquest to get the oil we need, a little reduction in democracy.

This lovely trip is turning into a horror trip, into Apocalypse Now. Part of the possessed soul is contorted with pain, screams in agony, rattles its chains, drags itself through the mud. But another part of the soul wants to continue with the trip. This internal schism—I want out, and I want to go on just as before—is part of our nature. I want out, but I am not willing to change for anything.

The demons speak. They have to speak if they are going to seduce, control, subjugate. We have to put up with the side effects, they tell us. After all, it is only ten percent of our population that has become mentally ill from the horror trip. The financial burden is not all that great; only about a fourth or fifth of our taxes go for military purposes. And as a return on that investment, we can kill every single Russian eleven times over. Isn't that terrific? If killing makes us secure, how much more secure overkill makes us!

Mark tells us three things about demons:
- They can be silenced.
- They know their enemies.
- They can be exorcised.

If the demons are to be silenced, then those who have renounced the horror trip have to become visible. If the demons do not know who we are, that means that we are remaining faceless, anonymous. It will not do any longer for us to pretend that we can quietly and peacefully go about our own business in an unoccupied country. It will not do any longer to pretend we do not know. We have all seen. Harrisburg and Seveso cannot be ignored.

As for the defense budget, we spend one out of three marks for defense out of an overall budget of about 59 billion marks. It has already been decided that we will spend more. A society that spends its money this way can correctly be called "militarized." A country with the largest military and police forces in Europe is—in the eyes of its neighbors at any rate—a militarized country, a country possessed by demons. We have seen what is going on, and we know how things will continue to go in the future. But have *we* become visible? Do the demons know *us*? Is there a peace movement *here*?

In the coming decades ecological problems and the development of alternative energy supplies will require all the resources, financial and intellectual, that we have. Every mark and every mind that we sacrifice to maintaining our stone-age relationships with other countries will be lost for solving the central problems facing humanity. The bombs that we are producing for later—just in case—are falling now. They are falling on the hungry, on the downtrodden, on those who demonstrate for ecological energy sources and are clubbed down for their pains.

We see what is happening. But have *we* become visible?

The demons know Jesus, and they know he is someone to be reckoned with. The NATO leaders know Holland, and they know they cannot just have their way there. The demons in their cruise missiles cannot just take over the whole country, cannot just drain off its air, its water, its energy. Whom do the demons know in our country? Whom do they fear? Who silences them? Where is Jesus if we "improve our defense posture"? Where is the church?

I cannot imagine that any demons "know" the Protestant Church in Germany. The Church has not made itself known. Nowadays the demons do not ask, "Do you want total war?" They call an arms buildup "modernization"; they speak of "stocking weapons" as if it were a matter of flour or sugar. They say "defense" when they mean offense. They feel threatened; their legs turn into spaghetti under them. The lights are going out, they whine; we have to arm ourselves!

If Jesus Christ were here in the Federal Republic of Germany in the 1980s, the demons would know him, and they would be afraid of him. Their opposition would not be just the mentally ill, not just the children of foreign workers, not just the unemployed, not just the helpless, the flipped out, the old, and the worn out. They would have to deal with someone who would stand in front of their military bases and say no, not for the third time in this century, not for oil or for anything else. Over my dead body, he would say.

He cast them out. He silenced them. He made himself known. The enemy knew his face. To believe in him does not mean just saying "terrific guy" but becoming like him. It means being known by the demons, being feared by them. Becoming militant, clear, and more and more fearless. With him, like him.

Why Are We Unable to Cast the Demon Out?

Thoughts on the Relationship between
Personal Faith and the Arms Buildup

What does it mean to be a Christian in a society that is becoming increasingly militarized? What does the NATO decision on the stationing of nuclear missiles in West Germany have to do with my life as a Christian? How does it concern me personally?

The Fear of Fear

True religious piety has a quality of wholeness about it. We seek a total relationship with life. Piety is the desire to give oneself completely, totally to the deepest meaning life has. As the Jewish daily prayer, the Shema Israel, puts it: "Listen, Israel: Yahweh our God is the one Yahweh. You shall love Yahweh your God with all your heart, with all your soul, with all your strength" (Deut. 6:4-5). Or in the variation that Jesus made on it: "You must love the Lord your God with all your heart, with all your soul, with all your mind and with all your strength" (Mark 12:30). It means total surrender to God's gift of life in the world, without denying or rejecting or repressing any of the strengths we have. To be religious means to give oneself to God, to take part in the movement of love in the world and to become love oneself.

This totality of devotion is impossible as long as we have to struggle with our unconscious emotions and do not permit ourselves to recognize them and transform them. To be whole means to be present with our feelings and with our understanding of the world. But how is this possible? We live, to put it succinctly, in a system of undernourishment and overkill. We profit from this system. The beast out of the sea rules over us.

23

1 John 4:18

Perfect love I read in the book
drives out fear
as long as I can remember I've wanted to know
what perfect love is and where it could be found
and stumbled over my own feet
whenever I think I can name all my fears
I find behind the last one a very last one
and from behind yesterday's very last fear
a new one creeps out
how stupid to stumble over your own feet
how cowardly not to know everyone in your own house
even imperfect love I tell myself
dispels and drives out
many fears but not enough
of your voice I could say at the very least
that it is determined and warm
and dispelling

Authentic theology has its roots in human experience. To state it the other way around: theology that denies or glosses over our most profound experiences is not genuine. It is merely an irrelevant leftover from tradition, preaching a kind of paper Christ, who, because he is not linked to our experience, is powerless to put us in touch with our feelings.

This paper Christ has, of course, nothing to say about the NATO decision to station nuclear weapons in Europe. The paper Christ is above such things. His place is in the other world.

But real faith has something to say about the reality we live in. It asks: How can we live whole lives in the midst of a death machine that we serve, pay for, and support? Whenever I try to look at reality and hear what it is telling me, my first reaction is to run away. I do not want to see it. I do not want to know anything about it. That is literally true: I cannot assimilate the figures, the number of atomic warheads, the number of square miles that can be laid waste, the accuracy of the delivery systems. I read these things and forget them immediately, not because I'm too stupid to remember them but because I really do not want to remember them. That knowledge makes life difficult; indeed, intolerable.

In this sense I am no better than my forebears in Nazi Germany who also claimed they "did not know." I am horrified, I want to forget, I have to repress, I have to repress my fear and put it aside as quickly as I can. I call this state of mind the fear of fear. It paralyzes me, blocks my powers, and makes a helpless thing of me, a person who cannot give herself up to the powerful current of love and cannot join in the struggle. The fear of fear finishes me off. Fear and the fear of fear stand between me and love.

1 John 4:18 says: "In love there can be no fear, for fear is driven out by perfect love." But this is not true of me. My love is too weak to cast out fear, and it is fear that dominates me, fear that tells me what to do. We live under a system of terror, and the military strategists who coined the phrase "the balance of terror" have revealed more than they meant to in that phrase. Living under a balance of terror makes us powerless and indecisive. We do not even have language adequate for attacking the terror that dominates us.

Many observers have called attention to the deceptive nature of the military vocabulary: a "preemptive strike" is one that destroys the enemy's nuclear weapons before a war has even begun. If a population is to be destroyed, the strategists speak of "countervalue." If nonmilitary targets are to be destroyed, the term is "counterforce." The word "counter" is used to emphasize the defensive character of our weaponry and disguise its aggressive character. That is the essence of the doublespeak that the propagandists for the arms buildup use. A counterstrike strategy has nothing to do with defense. The CDU (Christian Democratic Union) defense expert Wörner said in December 1979 that NATO had to redefine its mission. It is no longer enough, he said, to come to the aid of a NATO state that has been attacked. True defense requires a preventive first-strike capacity. True defense, in other words, is offense! To defend is to attack. The SPD (Social Democratic Party of Germany) denounced this formulation, but in practice our government is in agreement with what Wörner said: The stationing of 572 medium-range missiles in western Europe cannot be interpreted as a "defensive" measure, nor can Carter's Presidential Directive 59 of August 1980, which makes it clear that the United States considers a war conducted with atomic weapons conceivable and practicable.

What is new about this military policy is that it does away with that old, nebulous distinction between weapons that served "purely political" ends as deterrents and weapons that can be put into action. Atomic weapons were initially introduced only as a political threat. Today, this kind of deception no longer appears to be necessary.

How is it that we have arrived at this critical juncture? I shall try to give a brief historical survey of this development. After World War II, there was profound emotional and political opposition to the remilitarization of our country. The government began to introduce cosmetic linguistic changes. The military renamed its institutions. The ministry of war, war budget, and war research became ministry of defense, defense budget, and defense research. Today, the Pentagon spends $28 million each year on public relations—in other words, on psychological preparation for war. The CDU invented the term *nachrüsten* to replace *aufrüsten* (*aufrüsten* means "to build up armaments"; *nachrüsten* implies "arming in order to catch up with" another nation or power). Helmut Schmidt adopted the neologism. What it means in reality is a massive escalation in a nuclear arms race that is making no one more secure. Before the NATO decision in December 1979, which is one of the most important events in the last twenty years of the Federal Republic's history, Brezhnev withdrew 1,000 tanks and 20,000 troops from East Germany as a gesture of good will. He also offered to withdraw Soviet medium-range missiles provided no new NATO weapons would be stationed in western Europe. Moscow reduced the number of its bombers and missiles, cutting back the bombers, for example, from 725 to 525. NATO doubted the truth of these facts, but they have since been confirmed by leading U.S. politicians (see *Frankfurter Rundschau*, Aug. 12, 1980).

But none of that was enough to satisfy the West's security requirements and the requirements of Western industries, and the word *nachrüsten* was invented to distort and disguise this reality. The Peace Institute in Oslo and other neutral research centers have ascertained that in almost all fields of military technology the Soviet Union is about five years behind the Americans. American superiority and pressure from Russian military leaders have forced the Soviet Union into trying to catch up during the past twenty-five years. In 1960, for example, a nonexistent "missile gap" was invented; it resulted in increased missile production in the United States and played a role two years later in the Cuban missile crisis. Again and again a grossly exaggerated picture of Russia's military capability is drawn to frighten the American people into accepting the construction of new weapons of mass destruction. The result is a neurotic vicious circle. The militaristic projection of our worst fears brings us that much closer to seeing those fears realized.

But the language of fear makes us incapable of perceiving reality as it is. The fear of fear is like a demon that has power over us. I do not believe in demons that take the form of mysterious creatures flitting about in the air, but the demonic quality that I think is inherent in increasing militarism plays a major role in evoking the fear of fear. We find ourselves caught in a vicious circle, an inescapable cycle of fear and impotence that aids in the repression of anxiety. We repress the vital, life-saving forces of fear and give ourselves up to cynical or melancholic resignation. Impotence is one of the major features of our political and social life, and burdened as we are with our impotence and fear, it can be useful for us to review here once more the possible Christian positions on war and peace.

I personally am not committed to a position of total nonviolence.

My wishes

My wishes are like sparrows
impudent cacophonous birds
I've shooed them away many times
occasionally I've even downed one
with my analytical slingshot
and I've simply made up my mind
to live without sparrows
on a city courtyard for example
artificially lit and not particularly dirty
I can find pretty things
to buy and wrap I carry them
from one end of the subway
to the other
why not live my life in peace one day like the next
without these pests
innocently they come back
descend on me and occupy the land
how many times have I shooed them away
impudent cacophonous birds
you my wishes like sparrows

It may be that I can turn the other cheek to my enemies, but I cannot ask my sister in Argentina, whose son has been kidnapped and tortured to death, to do so. I have to look at this issue historically. When the Red Army liberated the death camps of Birkenau and Auschwitz in 1945, the sword was an instrument of hope and liberation. The question remains, though, whether this situation applies today. There are three traditional Christian attitudes toward war: pacifism, the doctrine of a just war, and the crusade.

The last of these I reject as un-Christian and inadmissable. It is no coincidence that the crusade ideology seized control of Christendom at about the same time persecution by the Inquisition did.

The question of how we can build peace is open to a number of different answers. Some answer it by following the example of the church fathers, who tried to define the criteria for a just war. In the context of their thinking, I would say, for instance, that the Cuban revolution and the Sandinista revolution in Nicaragua meet the criteria for just revolutions, revolutions that create a lasting peace based on justice.

The correspondence between Dan Berrigan and Ernesto Cardenal on Cardenal's role in the liberation movement in Nicaragua is an important document in the discussion of the Christian attitude toward peace. Cardenal gave up his position of nonviolence to join the Sandinistas. Dan Berrigan, a Jesuit and poet and a resistance fighter like his friend Cardenal, asked him how he could abandon the principle of nonviolence and take up arms: "Don't you realize that anyone who commits violence destroys not only his victims but himself as well?" Both of these men are my friends. Their commitment and their love of God are beyond any doubt for me. Both of them embody something of that mystical and revolutionary spirit that we all need.

Ernesto was in exile when I met him in 1979, and he said to me that he could not answer Dan's question because he loved him too much. "But you know," he added, "Dan doesn't know what revolution is."

Cardenal, who has become minister of culture in Nicaragua in the meantime, subordinated his work for peace to his duty to see justice done. What we in the First World can learn from this discussion is to remain open to both these impulses in the peace movement, not to let either option assume the force of an absolute. Here in our country we are not involved in a peasants' and fishermen's war of liberation against a ruling clique. Our situation is that all of us, young and old alike, are forced to be accomplices to a gigantic death machine and that we have not been asked what we prefer to do with our time, our intelligence, and our money. We are possessed by a demon that is located neither in Washington nor in Moscow but rather in the very nature of the arms industry itself.

Why Not We?

I want to cite a Bible story here to illustrate how the fear of fear can be overcome:

> When they rejoined the disciples they saw a large crowd around him and some scribes arguing with them. The moment they saw Jesus the whole crowd were struck with amazement and ran to greet him. "What are you arguing about with them?" he asked. A man answered him from the crowd, "Master, I have brought my son to you; there is a spirit of dumbness in him, and when it takes hold of him it throws him to the ground, and he foams at the mouth and grinds his teeth and goes rigid. And I asked your disciples to cast it out and they were unable to." "You faithless generation," he said to them in reply. "How much longer must I be with you? How much longer must I put up with you? Bring him to me." They brought the boy to him, and as soon as the spirit saw Jesus it threw the boy into convulsions, and he fell to the ground and lay writhing there, foaming at the mouth. Jesus asked the father, "How long has this been happening to him?" "From childhood," he replied, "and it has often thrown him into the fire and into the water, in order to destroy him. But if you can do anything, have pity on us and help us." "If you can?" retorted Jesus. "Everything is possible for anyone who has faith." Immediately the father of the boy cried out, "I do have faith. Help the little faith I have!" And when Jesus saw

how many people were pressing around him, he rebuked the unclean spirit. "Deaf and dumb spirit," he said, "I command you: come out of him and never enter him again." Then throwing the boy into violent convulsions it came out shouting, and the boy lay there so like a corpse that most of them said, "He is dead." But Jesus took him by the hand and helped him up, and he was able to stand. When he had gone indoors his disciples asked him privately, "Why were we unable to cast it out?" "This is the kind," he answered, "that can only be driven out by prayer" [Mark 9:14–29].

Let us ask the same question that the disciples asked after Jesus had healed he epileptic boy: Why cannot we cast out the militaristic demon? Why not *we*? The whole story deals with the question of powerlessness and comes back to the question of faith. "Everything is possible for anyone who has faith," Jesus says. This sentence is at the heart of Jesus' message of liberation. But is it true? This claim seems to be at odds with all our experience. During these recent years of growing inflation and oppression, these hard times with their increased hunger in the Third World and increased weapons buildups in the First, I have heard many people say: "Nothing is possible! There is nothing we can do." No one has asked us whether we wanted to be able to kill every man, woman, and child in Russia eleven times over instead of just nine. What can we do about that? "Everything is possible," Jesus says.

Most of the people in the Bible story do not believe this. First there are the disciples who could not cast out the evil spirit and were unable to heal the boy. The scribes had attacked them before Jesus arrived. It is easy to imagine what the scribes said. For instance: "You are no better than our forefathers. You can't change anything. It doesn't make the least bit of difference whether you're here or not. How can your leader claim the kingdom of God is here if demons still plague us?"

Instead of consoling his friends, Jesus is critical of them and has nothing but harsh words for them. He calls them faithless, suggesting that they are allied with death, not with life; dependent on the death machine, integrated into the kingdom of death, dominated and governed by the powers of death. Being as powerless as they are is a kind of death. If this interpretation is right, what is our situation?

And then there is the epileptic boy himself who has been possessed by this demon for years on end. The boy has tried to kill himself several times. "[The spirit] has often thrown him into the fire and into the water, in order to destroy him." The suicide attempts are another expression of helplessness. Jesus listens to this report of depression, of demonic possession. The case is, as we would say, a hopeless one. Or, to use more objective, medical language, we would say that the boy is incurable. But Jesus never indulges in this kind of talk.

And, finally, there is the father of the epileptic boy. The father asks Jesus to have pity, and Jesus criticizes him with biting scorn. The father says: "But if you can do anything, have pity on us and help us." Jesus seem to feel insulted by this if-you-can attitude. He repeats the words "if you can " and rejects the view that gave rise to them. "Everything is possible for anyone who has faith." Why do so many people talk the way the boy's father does? Because they are unsure, helpless, and in doubt about their own capabilities. They have been living with their own weakness for so long that they cannot believe in their own power and strength. Why do they lack what Jesus calls faith? Why do we not have what Jesus calls faith? Why can we not cast the demon out? Why do we go on living endlessly in fear of fear? Why are we possessed by the militaristic demon and, if we are honest with ourselves, almost constantly depressed? The turning point in this story is when the father cries out: "I do have faith. Help the little faith I have!"

We are here to work for peace. Let us at least try to be like the boy's father. Let us renounce the position of the disciples, the one that means having no faith and no power. Let us adopt instead the father's position, which, caught between doubt and fear and resignation on the one hand and faith and struggle on the other, takes a small step toward faith. There is hope in the father's cry. If we cry out loudly enough, there will be hope in our cry, too. Why can we not cast the demon out? Faith means participating in God's creative and healing power. It means being at one with the power of life. It means feeling within ourselves the same power to heal and create, and to act on that power. It means organizing resistance against death.

Faith and struggle are one. The fact that the demon is still among us, sucking our blood, is a concrete political issue and at the same time a religious and spiritual issue. What does it mean to cast a demon out? It means first of all to call it by name, to understand how its sphere of influence is constituted and what the principles are by which it operates.

One of the weaknesses of traditional pacifism is, I think, that it is often unable to untangle the complex intertwinings of seemingly unrelated themes. The demon we are struggling with is not just bloodthirsty militarism or simply a need for security coupled with a disregard for human life. Militarism is an inevitable by-product of the economic system in which we live. If the peace movement wants to go beyond mere moral admonition, it will have to offer a more comprehensive analysis than it does now, one that will show how the fates of, say, three human beings—a Turkish worker in Berlin-Kreuzberg, a single mother in a Brazilian slum, and a bank president in Frankfurt—are interrelated in a global context. The conditions of these three persons' lives are affected—indeed, dictated—by growing militarism.

In the first two months of 1980, military-industrial stocks gained tremendously in value. On January 31, 1980, the *Frankfurter Allgemeine Zeitung* published an ad that advised readers to invest 25 percent of their income in the arms industry. Why? The United States had increased its military budget by $16 billion. That set the ball rolling, and sooner or later all the NATO countries and other countries would follow suit. There is no need to decode or interpret here. Everything is stated in the clear text of economics. Political questions are not even mentioned. And this is only one example of the socio-economic dynamics involved.

Calling the demon by name also means understanding the historical background of the present arms buildup. For thirty-five years the United States has based its foreign policy on American military superiority and economic strength. The United States would not dream of relinquishing this superiority even if retaining it meant a risk of atomic war. After World War II, America needed export markets for its surplus production. But very few countries had the money to pay for American goods, and Washington created an economic and military program, the so-called Pax Americana, to correct that situation. This program had two objectives:

1) From 1945 to 1975, America put up $170 million in loans and guarantees to stabilize the economies of its allies.

2) The economic plan was backed up by a military program that guaranteed to governments that chose to live under the terms of the Pax Americana that they would be protected not only from attacks from without but also—and above all—from subversion by their own population.

Without American weapons and military training, the successful military coup of 1963 against the government of the Dominican Republic could never have been staged. Nor could the Bolivian government have been ousted by General Rene Barrientos, or the Brazilian government by General Castelo Branco, or the Allende government in Chile by General Pinochet.

Countries such as Saudi Arabia, Jordan, Korea, the Philippines, and most Latin American countries would have had popular revolutions long ago if the Americans had not supported the governments there. The raison d'être for the massive military machine and the economic aid is to keep governments in power that are friendly to American interests. Anyone who acts contrary to American interests is not allowed to come to power.

When the civil war against the military junta in El Salvador began, an American politician said: "We've lost Nicaragua. We can't afford to lose El Salvador too."

The Pax Americana is a peace that is based on injustice and oppression. It guarantees the exploiters the freedom to exploit, and wherever this freedom is threatened by a people that defines its freedom differently, U.S. military forces intervene and protect the interests of the multinational or U.S. concerns that have often formed alliances with the ruling elites in Third World countries. Military power is thus an element of a neocolonial economic system. And every escalation in the arms race has to be understood not only as an escalation in the cold war between East and West but also as an escalation in the war that the rich are waging against the poor, the northern hemisphere is waging against the southern.

"The bombs are falling now." Our defense system is not engaged in preparing for a military conflict in the future; it is engaged in a war right now, a war we are living in, a war in which 15,000 people die every day because they have nothing to eat. Our world has enough food to satisfy everyone's needs, but an economic war is taking place, forced on 800 million people who live in a condition that Robert McNamara described as absolute poverty. For them malnutrition and illiteracy are the norm. Disease and destitution are on the increase. Infant mortality is high, life expectancy is low. We have to realize that it is not overpopulation or a shortage of natural resources that forces these millions to live on the verge of starvation and leaves their children mentally retarded for lack of protein.

The bombs are falling now.

The economic war goes on. Brazil is experiencing a growth in gross national product that is referred to as an economic miracle. The only problem is that the poor are hungrier than they have ever been. Black beans, a basic staple in the diet of the poor, are not being raised anymore; instead, soy beans are being raised for export. In some of the most fertile areas in South America strawberries and orchids are cultivated. In the interest of interlocking economic ties, economic dependencies are being systematically created throughout the entire world. This amounts to the deliberate impoverishment of even those countries that not long ago were able to produce enough food for themselves. This creation of dependency, this robbing and impoverishment of other parts of the world, is a consequence of our economic expansion, the security of which we have to insure by building up our military capabilities.

The bombs are falling now, not at some indeterminate time in the future. In hopes of forcing the Soviet Union to arm itself to death, we are arming the Third World to death. Instead of giving it the help it needs, we continue to subject it to an economic system whose patent objective is to make the rich richer and the poor poorer.

When we in West Germany opted for cannons instead of butter in December 1979, we made a choice that also affected our own quality of life adversely. We have to train and employ fewer doctors, nurses, social workers, and teachers. We have to retrench socially so that we can expand militarily. But this affects the poor in the rest of the world in yet another way. West Germany is among the leading exporters of weapons; here again we are exporting death to the poorest of the poor.

The bombs are falling now in still another sense: they are falling dead center into the scientific community and destroying the minds and spirits of researchers. Chemical warfare was outlawed by the international community long ago, but new programs for the production of chemical weapons are still being put into effect. Research scientists in the United States are developing a so-called nerve gas that is invisible and odorless and takes effect within fifteen minutes. Headache, vomiting, and muscle spasms quickly lead to coma and death. It is estimated that more than 400,000 scientists and technicians are employed by the arms industry, and this does not take into account those whose research is utilized indirectly to increase the capacity to kill.

We must not overlook the significance of this destruction of human reason or fail to see how disastrous is this degradation of human intelligence to mere instrumental intelligence. If science and the search for truth become appendages of the military machine, then the so-called freedom of research is limited to the interests of the security ideology. The bombs have already fallen, and they have crippled a rational capability that used to be guided by an interest in the welfare of the entire human family. Under the pretext of scientific neutrality and in a realm supposedly untouched by politics, the capacity for truth of the very people who are the embodiment of human intelligence in our time is being extinguished.

In West Germany, the military establishment is no longer one of those necessary evils we would rather do without; moral justification for it is no longer necessary. It is becoming an ever increasing presence in all our social institutions, in industrial production, in the economy, in political theory, in social life, in education, in psychology. In all these areas, the influence of militarism is growing. In December 1980, the minister of defense asked of the conference of the ministers of culture that "issues bearing on security and peace policy be given more attention in the schools" (*Frankfurter Rundschau*, Dec. 6, 1980). The order in which "security" and "peace" appear speaks for itself. The critical attitude that the young have toward the *Bundeswehr* has been cited as the justification for this new school subject.

The term "peace policy" occurs less and less frequently in the language of government officials; "peace" alone does not adequately define the political objective our government has in mind. The correct expression is "security and peace policy," and the minister of defense has made clear in an interview exactly what this expression means: "We [the government of the Federal Republic] have to be the prime movers in the Western alliance when it comes to maintaining our defense capability and to exploring possibilities for arms limitations" (*Deutsches Allgemeines Sonntagsblatt*, May 27, 1979). As if we had not been "prime movers" enough in this century for what the defense minister calls—in inimitable rhetoric—the "maintenance of our defense capability," a capability that, despite the largest defense budget in the history of the Federal Republic, is supposedly threatened and weakened. It is not our capability for peace that is presented as underdeveloped but our defense capability, our weaponry power.

Blessed are the Peacemakers

But it is not enough just to call the demon by name. We have to organize resistance, resistance that begins with the formation of cells and groups that oppose the demon and challenge it. We have to fight to reclaim the dignity that is ours through participation in power. This is what Jesus had in mind when he praised the resistance fighters of his time and called them "peacemakers." "Happy the peacemakers; they shall be called sons of God" (Matt. 5:9). Both these expressions—peacemakers and sons of God—were completely inappropriate for a wandering Galilean radical to use when addressing a handful of fishermen. The word "peacemaker," *eirenepoios*, was stamped onto Caesar's coins and was one of those flattering titles the Roman rulers liked to be addressed by. Another of those titles was "son of God" or "son of the highest." In the Roman Empire of that time the emperors were the only ones who could be called sons of God because they were the peacemakers and maintained the Pax Romana.

When Jesus used these terms to describe ordinary people his usage reflected two fundamental ideas. One is that peace is not made from above by traveling diplomats or powerful emperors. Peace is made by ordinary men and women. And the other is that it is right and proper to call these ordinary people sons and daughters of the highest because they participate in God's power.

This brings us back again to the gospel narrative about faith and power, faithlessness and powerlessness. Jesus rejects the father's "if-you-can" hypothesis. He defines faith in terms of "everything is possible." Let us consider once again what theology the story of the epileptic boy and his father contains. What does it mean, in the light of this story, to have faith?

When I was studying theology I was taught that faith means trust in God. But now it seems inadequate to me to say that faith means trust because that might mean that the one who is trusted has all the power and strength, and those who trust have all the weakness. Now I prefer to think that "everything is possible for anyone who has faith." This suggests more than a child's trust in a strong father. It suggests instead that we finally become adults. Faith becomes actual where strength and weakness come together. Faith means becoming the image of God, being created in his image.

It is not important that we see human beings as having a physical likeness with God. What is important is that we regard ourselves as people who can act as God does—that is, in a powerful, creative, life-giving way. To be created in the image of God means to participate in God's power. It means becoming a co-creator. These are not idealistic or over optimistic terms. They reflect experiences that we have had ourselves and that have to do with the very heart of our lives, experiences such as sexual joy and the gratification of work that we find fulfilling. We have these experiences all too rarely, but that does not make them any the less real. When these aspects of adult life work out well for us, we come to know ourselves anew and our bond with life deepens. In one of his famous remarks, Freud defined health as the capacity to love and to work. What he meant is the participation in the power of life that is denied to the majority of people in our society. When the Bible says that we are created in the image of God, it means that we are able to share in that power.

From this idea of being created in the image of God, Jewish religious tradition developed a doctrine of the imitation of God in human conduct. Imitating God means doing very simple things: clothing the naked, as God made clothes for Adam and Eve; burying the dead, as God buried Moses; feeding the hungry, as God

I saw you

I saw you with my own eyes
your hair was standing on end around your face
your eyes were wide open as if you knew
that the rule of injustice would collapse
tomorrow at the latest
your hand grasped the concepts
and played with them unhurriedly
you mixed them tossed them in the air
and caught them again
I saw you with my own eyes
among a group of seven or eight
you were drawing them into something
that was contagious and made people laugh
how beautiful movements become
when we organize resistance to the rule of injustice
how beautiful the fighter's hands

fed Elijah with the help of the ravens. It means creating justice and not languishing in powerlessness any longer. We are created in God's image because we can act like God and transcend the given. We can create justice and therefore peace.

All things are possible, Jesus says. I read this story about the epileptic boy in the light of our existence as images of God, but I know from some theological commentaries I have read that there are interpretations of this story that run completely counter to my own. Some theologians assign the power to work miracles to Christ alone, stressing his ability to heal where all our efforts are in vain. Other theologians stress the all-too-familiar weakness of human beings and our inability to do what God's all-powerful hand alone can accomplish. Some preachers cite this story to make the gap between God and us, between Christ and us, appear even wider. I cannot accept this interpretation. I mention this model of "Christ accomplished miracles/we can accomplish nothing" because it plays such an important role in discussion within the church between those who think an arms buildup is necessary and those who want to live without the protection of weapons. A theology that regards human beings as powerless will favor an arms buildup to protect national interests.

I think what the teller of our story wanted to achieve was to encourage the disciples to become like Jesus: if they had faith, they could work miracles just as he did; all things would be possible to them. That is unquestionably Jesus' intention. He wants to release us from powerlessness, from our love of death. He wants to set us free—that is, he wants to make us capable of using our own powers. If we were free and powerful, peace would be possible; disarmament would be possible; there could be justice on earth, and its riches would be available to all.

Christ was not given to us so that we could feel weak and powerless. He is not "up there," and we "down here." His power is not undivided; such power would be an evil that an individual could monopolize for himself or herself to turn against others. Christ's power is the benevolent strength that grows when it is shared with others. It is shared power in which we have a share. Even Christ could not heal the epileptic boy without the boy's father. He needed the father's faith. He depends on others. What good would a healing be if the boy's father were not radically transformed? And how can peace come about if we cannot learn to think differently?

All things are possible for God through those who believe in him. Do we belong to that company? If so, why have we not been able to cast out that immense demon that dominates our lives? Who really believes in the peace of God, in the continuation of Jesus' miracles, in the possibility of healing, in God's continuing creation, through us, of peace and justice? Do we believe in God?

No, we believe in armaments. Our lives demonstrate again and again that not all things are possible. We cannot disarm because of the Russians! And because we cannot disarm, we cannot feed the hungry. Instead, we have to keep food prices up by destroying our surplus food production. Nothing is possible if we cannot escape from the vicious circle made up of fear, neurotic need for security, the fear of fear, and a sense of weakness.

Being a Christian in these times means becoming a resistance fighter. It means developing and practicing resistance on all levels of our lives. This resistance starts with refusing to buy, give, or put up with toy soldiers, toy guns, toy tanks—and I include among such toys the medals that our army suddenly feels it needs again. Resistance includes fearless exposure of just what our so-called security policy really means. It includes refusing to participate either as a soldier or a nurse in an atomic war, refusing to "do one's duty" still another time. Resistance also means acts of civil disobedience, such as tax resistance, the blocking of weapons shipments, and other similar actions that opponents of the Vietnam "conflict" developed in America.

We have to move toward the objectives of peacemaking a step at a time. Living without weapons is a long-range goal and, in the best sense of the term, a utopian demand. The demon can be cast out. It does not have to dominate us, torture us, and drive us to suicide for all time. But we have to work toward this great objective by individual steps. The Dutch peace movement's demand was: "Free the world of atomic weapons! Begin in the Netherlands!" We have to reveal for what it is the government's illusion or lie—I shall not presume to say which—that we can negotiate better through and after an arms buildup. As if it would be a simple matter to rid ourselves of those 572 Cruise and Pershing II missiles once we have them! But we will not be able to achieve this medium-range goal of

41

preventing implementation of the NATO decision unless we first reach the short-range one of developing in our country a movement comparable to the Dutch peace movement.

Our first step is to convert others to become active agents for peace. We have to learn to join together and repoliticize ourselves in the light of the most important issue of our time. To do this, we need to feel within ourselves the strength that will help us overcome powerlessness. Only together can we learn faith. We need to attend to the experience that older persons have of what an arms buildup has led to twice before in this century. We have to attend to the elemental fear the younger generation feels—the fear that our earth will be destroyed. To make our stand against death, we need every last person in our country. All things are possible, Jesus said. It is time that we start taking him at his word.

In reagan's country

What on earth are you doing in reagan's country
my friends in germany ask me
you have no business there
but it isn't true
that history belongs to the victors

what on earth are you doing in a marble palace
built with rockefeller billions
that they call a church
but it isn't true
that the bible belongs to the militarists

what on earth are you doing in the midst of the war
the rich wage against the poor
on the side of those with power
but it isn't true
that the occupied countries
belong to the occupiers

the truth is my friends
that the foxes have holes
and the birds have nests
but he hath not
where to lay his head
only a few friends
for whose sake he stayed

What we need the ogre for

Since 1974 nato has been following a new scenario in its maneuvers
foreign armies from the east attack us
as they so often have before
starving unemployed workers inside the country
make common cause with them
that is new
in the war games that keep us prepared for all eventualities

To crucify

To crucify
      to execute—to dispose of—to get out of the way—
      to put in solitary—to leave an electric light on day
          and night—
      to sentence for life—to order special treatment
to crucify
      to do away with—to destroy—to liquidate—
      to wipe out—to purge—to expel—
      to straighten out—to streamline—to urban renew—to
          evict—
      to threaten eviction—to do someone in
to crucify
      to provide no place to live—to keep from learning a
          trade—
      to put in an institution—to kick out of a resort—
      to be offended in our esthetic sensibilities—
      to be unable to bear the sight of —
      to not want our neighborhood ruined—to gas
to crucify
      to send to a state welfare home—to turn into a
          criminal—
      to encourage dependency—to addict—
      to foster neurosis—to intimidate—
      to stupefy—to pull the rug from under—
      to cow—to brutalize
to crucify
      to forget—to conceal—to not want to make a fuss
          about—
      to repress—to not have known about it—
      to consider it an isolated case—
      to call it inevitable—to let it happen

to crucify
     to bump off—to silence for good—
     to bind and gag—
     to deprive of language—
     to make deaf and dumb—to plug the ears—
     to put off with false hopes—to blindfold—to gouge out
         eyes—
     to turn into consumers—
     to blind—to stifle
to crucify
     to prepare the final solution—
     to make conform to the values of society—
     to adjust—to execute—

And on the other side of the border

And on the other side of the border
you realize that don't you
lives an ogre who is much worse
totally undemocratic
he is growing fat
on the possessions and taxes
on the bodies and time and life
on the spirit and soul and research
of the poor who are his subjects

Unrestrained by a free democratic social order
you must never forget that
he is growing unchecked
and according to our latest information
his waist is one inch
larger than that of our ogre
though his live weight is
one quarter pound less
and that right on our border

So that we have no choice
but to take appropriate measures
to end the emaciation
of our native ogre
we have no choice but
to catch up by building him up

Democratize, Don't Militarize

In December 1979 NATO decided to station medium-range nuclear missiles in Europe. This decision is one of the most important events of the 1970s and '80s for every one of us. It marked the beginning of a new escalation in the arms race. It means:

in terms of world politics

The poor will become poorer still. The industrialized countries are spending thirty times more money for arms than they are for aid to developing countries. Every day more than two billion marks (approx. $800 million) are spent for the destruction of humanity. These bombs and missiles are not going to fall sometime in the future. They are falling now. On the starving peoples of the world.

in terms of the economy

Our extremely high standard of living in West Germany will be defended by military means. The slogan "a nation without territory" that was used to prepare the way for the Nazis' world war now reads: "a nation without oil." We need the arms buildup to insure that we can continue to import our most important source of energy. And if it must be, we will resort to force.

in strategic terms

The old conception of NATO as a defensive alliance has been abandoned. Spokesmen for the CDU (Christian Democratic Union) have stated this openly. Representatives of the other parties have agreed to it implicitly by their acceptance of the NATO

48

decision. The new weapons are offensive, not defensive, weapons. Europe—or at least Germany, both East and West—has become the new battlefield.

in terms of domestic politics

We shall have to scale down our social programs in order to build up our military forces. Our society is being militarized through and through. The *Bundeswehr* is being celebrated and honored with medals; its public image is being refurbished. Those who work for peace encounter discrimination. The consciences of those who care for the elderly and the sick, not of those who learn to kill, are subject to question and scrutiny.

As Christians we should not ask our political parties the rhetorical question: "Do you want peace?" The question we should ask is: "Do you want to serve the cause of peace with more or with fewer arms?" Some politicians argue for an arms buildup. Others think they can arm and disarm at the same time. As followers of Jesus, the only path we can follow is to demand limited, unilateral disarmament.

The arms buildup arises from a "spirit of fear." But "God's gift was not a spirit of timidity, but the Spirit of power and love and self-control" (2 Tim. 1:7). Fear leads to a neurotic need for security that can never be satisfied and that, in league with other interests, always increases. Faith leads us to risk peace.

Dietrich Bonhoeffer wrote in 1934: "How will peace come about? By a multilateral 'peaceful' arms buildup designed to ensure peace? No! The path of security will not give us peace. We have to take a chance with peace. It demands great risk, and it can never be guaranteed. To ask for security means to be suspicious, and this suspicion leads once again to war."

The spirit of Christ is a spirit in which we can take the risk of peace—by renouncing, unilaterally if need be, the use of force; by limited disarmament; by democratizing our society rather than militarizing it.

The security and peace policy of the federal republic of germany

A little dog is standing at the door
the ogre has him on a leash

First of all security says the master
then you'll get a nice big bone

First of all the silent scentless nerve gas
fifteen minutes after you puke you pass out
then I'll do some research for you on combatting famine

The little dog on the ogre's leash
just lifts its leg it doesn't even bark

Dinosaurs

The dinosaurs
didn't change
in the last 30,000 years of their existence
their weapons technology was too good
thanks to their armored hides
and the long reach of their forelegs
no enemy had a chance
against them

They also seem to have been familiar with
the theory of the preemptive strike
their need for security
must have been so overwhelming
that intelligence and feeling
had no room to develop
in their relatively small brains

Living without Weapons
or
Securing the Peace?

*What the atomic bomb represents is the negation of
humankind. Not only because there is a danger that it will
destroy all humanity but primarily because it renders the
specifically human qualities of courage, patience,
intelligence, and enterprise useless and ineffective.*
                                                    —Jean-Paul Sartre

When Jean-Paul Sartre made this observation the atomic bomb
was still in its earliest stages. Every one of the 572 nuclear missiles
that NATO is planning to station in Europe has forty times the
destructive power of the bomb dropped in Hiroshima.

How are Christians reacting to the present threat to peace? When
I was traveling in England a while ago speaking on disarmament
issues, the first question that audiences would ask me was: "Are
you a unilateralist?" Public discussion in England, as in Holland
and Scandinavia, has progressed a bit further than it has in West
Germany. There are two major proposals on disarmament:
unilateral disarmament as a demonstration of good will or bilateral
disarmament arrived at by negotiation. The wider question under
dispute is whether the cause of peace is better served by an
increased arms buildup, by developing new weapons technologies,
such as chemical warfare, by deterrence, and by threatening one's
opponent, or whether it is not more in the interest of peace to
forego unilaterally the development of new weapons, such as the
medium-range missiles that NATO has decided to deploy in
western Europe. We have to realize that in the context of weapons
technology the seemingly harmless word "development" includes
research, testing, production, training personnel in the use of a

given weapons system, stockpiling, and sales to other countries. How are we going to live with the atomic bombs that are already in place? The peace debate has split the English Labor Party and even the German SPD. It has also split the Protestant Church in Germany. Protestants who are committed to "living without weapons" oppose others whose main concern is to "secure the peace."

This debate is by no means new. The Heidelberg Theses of 1959 stated that it was possible from a Christian point of view to serve peace with weapons as well as without them. But now, with peace less secure than ever before, this "seesaw formulation," as Heinrich Albertz has called it, has come under renewed scrutiny. At its congress in Nairobi in 1975, the World Council of Churches called on Christians to combat militarism. This appeal was not widely publicized in West Germany. The appeal urged churches "to stress their willingness to live without the protection of weapons and to work for effective disarmament."

To date, about ten thousand Protestants in the Federal Republic have acted on this appeal by joining the action group "Living without Weapons." The group urges individuals to make a personal declaration to forego the protection of weapons. This program, which is simply formulated and has therefore been criticized for being "naive," has since been elaborated upon and now reflects the position of neutral peace researchers who base their hopes for humanity's survival on the willingness of concerned individuals to initiate unilateral, step-by-step disarmament. The renunciation of violence is at the heart of this Christian position. As Helmut Gollwitzer has said, "If we do not abolish the arms race, it will abolish us."

In the meantime, the opposing camp has rallied under the slogan "Securing the Peace" and is speaking out in favor of an arms buildup. Prominent theologians such as Wolfhart Pannenberg, Gerhard Ebeling, and Heinz Zahrnt have joined together with a group of lay persons and scholars who feel, on the basis of their Christian responsibility, that unilateral disarmament is wrong and a threat to peace. Unlike the adherents of "Living without Weapons," they think that the Federal Republic of Germany, given the present state of military technology, could be successfully defended and would survive a nuclear war. They also think that an arms buildup and negotiations to end the arms race can go on simultaneously. A Christian, they say—and this brings us to the difference of theological opinion underlying this controversy —takes into account not only the commandment of love but also the power of sin, the human being's intractable—and often brutal—will to power. This will to power cannot always be disarmed by the force of love, they contend.

These opposing theses on the disarmament issue are rooted in two fundamentally different theological positions, positions that differ in their conception of reality, in their understanding of what Christ means for us, in their understanding of what human beings are capable of. The peace issue is a touchstone that reveals how Christians understand Christianity today. And the differences in this understanding are far more important than traditional differences of denomination.

Is love for one's enemy sheer nonsense, or is it a realistic commandment for our time? Should we try to live according to the Sermon on the Mount, or is security—now as before—our highest value? Is the renunciation of violence a form of surrender and an irresponsible act toward those who are without protection? Is it possible to live without violence, as Christ did, or are we obliged to prepare the most massive act of violence that human history has yet conceived of—namely, nuclear holocaust—in order to combat the sin and lust for power of others? Can we, as Christians, put our faith—and that means our money, our research, and our vital energies—in nuclear missiles? Or is that idolatry, as Bishop Scharf has called it?

How did Jesus live, and what was the essence of his message? Did he want to drive home for us how powerful sin is, particularly the sin of others, or did he in fact believe in that other reality, the capacity of nonviolent love to transform the world?

And what can we as Christians say about God? Is he a tyrant who makes use of violence? Can we become soldiers in his name? Does he talk in terms of deterrence and potential destruction? Is it not true instead that God, in the most unilateral way imaginable, renounced the use of violence when he became flesh, when he became the man from Nazareth who was without property or weapons? What is the ultimate reality we choose to guide our lives by: power, threats, and violence, or liberation and love?

I cannot take a neutral position between those who want to "secure the peace" and those who want to "live without weapons." It is hard for me to see the Bible as saying anything other than God disarmed unilaterally. He renounced violence unilaterally and without waiting for us. It seems impossible to me for a Christian to use nuclear weapons. But in a Protestant church there is no body that has final authority in matters of doctrine. There is no Vatican, no church leadership that can establish legally binding policy for everyone.

The controversy I have described here has to be argued out by everyone, and everyone has to be able to follow his or her own conscience without fear of repression. Martin Luther thought that a Christian congregation had the right to judge in matters of doctrine and life, and he envisioned discussion of such matters taking place in a dialogue free of domination. The Bible provides guidance for the conscience, but is ambiguous in this area, providing examples that support both violence and nonviolence. What this means is that no citizen, man or woman, young or old, can sidestep these issues. They cannot be left to military experts or to theologians whose thinking is in keeping with the government's position. Questions of conscience cannot be relegated to others. And there are a few Christians who will not cease to ask their fellow citizens in the words of Ezekiel: "Why are you so anxious to die?" (18:31).

To All Christians

Document

We have become accustomed to saying:
A strong defense helps us maintain peace
   —but does it not threaten the lives of us all?
A strong defense creates jobs
   —but does it not take bread from millions who are starving?
A strong defense helps us contain violence
   —but does it not give rise to wars and terror?
We have hoped for disarmament
   —but are not ever more perfect weapons systems being
     developed?
We have said that it is worth 2.80 marks out of every 10 marks that
we pay in taxes to be secure
   —but do not our war taxes keep increasing the danger of war?

In view of this situation the fifth general assembly of the World
Council of Churches that met in Nairobi in 1975 urged this policy
on its 271 member churches:
   "The church should stress its willingness to live without the
protection of weapons and should take meaningful steps toward an
effective disarmament program."
   In accepting and propagating this policy we declare:
   "I am willing to live without the protection of military arms. I
will work in our country for the political realization of peace
without weapons."
   "If you do not stand by me, you will not stand at all" (Isa. 7:9).
   "But now in Christ Jesus, you that used to be so far apart from
us have been brought very close, by the blood of Christ. For he is
the peace between us, and has made the two into one and broken

down the barrier which used to keep them apart, actually destroying in his own person the hostility caused by the rules and decrees of the Law. This was to create one single New Man in himself out of the two of them and by restoring peace through the cross, to unite them both in a single Body and reconcile them with God. In his own person he killed the hostility. Later he came to bring the good news of peace, *peace to you who were far away and peace to those who were near at hand (Ps. 8:6)"* (Eph. 2:13–17).

LIVING WITHOUT WEAPONS—a committee of Pro Oekumene

This appeal has the support of:
    The Religious Brotherhood of Württemberg
    The International Fellowship of Reconciliation (IFOR)
    The Protestant Committee to Assist Conscientious Objectors
       and Workers in Alternative Service (EAK)
    The Convent of Württemberg Assistant Ministers
    The German Mennonite Peace Committee (DMFK)
    Church and Peace
    Religious Society of Friends, Pyrmont Yearly Meeting

Unilateralism   or god's vulnerability

Why are you so one-sided
people often ask me
so blind and so unilateral
I sometimes ask in return
are you a christian
if you don't mind my asking

And depending on the answer I remind them
how one-sidedly and without guarantees
god made himself vulnerable in christ
where would we end up
I offer for consideration
if god insisted on bilateral agreements
with you and me
who welsh on treaties
by resorting to various tricks
where would we end up
if god insisted on bilateral agreements
before he acted

Then I remind them
that god didn't come in an armored car
and wasn't born in a bank
and gave up the old miracle weapons
thunder and lightning and heavenly hosts
one-sidedly
palaces and kings and soldiers
were not his way when he
decided unilaterally
to become a human being
which means to live without weapons

Military Draft for Women?

A military draft for women? Women in the German army? A new debate is upon us. At the end of last year Defense Minister Apel touched on the subject of women in the military. He was asked: "When will there be women in the army?" And his reply was: "That will depend on the progress of public debate on this question and perhaps, too, on the anticipated shortage of personnel, which could become critical for the *Bundeswehr* from 1985 on."

The question was cleverly stated. It did not address the basic issue of *whether* women should be drafted at all; it took that point for granted and simply asked when will this start happening. That is no coincidence. We are being prepared to accept the idea of obligatory military service for women. It is being introduced to us in small doses in hopes that we shall gradually become accustomed to it. The reason that is served up to justify it is the drop in birthrate that followed after the introduction of the pill. Those years with low birthrates could leave us with a shortage of soldiers in the near future.

Those same years also supply the finance minister with his favorite argument against adequate financing for our schools. I have two daughters of school age, and the argument I hear time and again when I complain about the shortage of teachers, the dropping of courses, and overcrowded classrooms is always the same: the pill and the low birthrates it occasioned. That is why young teachers with no jobs are not hired and why the children going to school now are being cheated out of the instruction they are entitled to.

Our society remains unwilling to solve these questions, which number among the most central and critical ones we face. The years with low birthrates have to take the blame for less education and increasing militarization.

Women in the military seems to be a popular idea in the economic sector, too. Management organizations are talking up obligatory military duty for women as a miraculous solution to unemployment, from which women, of course, suffer more than men.

Thus, the old socialist saying that women represent capital's reserve army, which can always be called up for active duty in an emergency, applies here in a new and surprisingly literal sense.

The issue becomes all the more interesting when we note that the military's demands are receiving support from a quarter that no doubt causes our military leaders more dismay than pleasure —namely, a segment of the feminist movement. Alice Schwarzer was quoted as saying that she could not favor denying a woman the career and retirement pay of a four-star general. These feminists intend to sue—as a political provocation—for the *right to be a soldier*. This position is shared by some women who do not necessarily feel that becoming a four-star general is a desirable goal in life but who ask nonetheless how women, who up to now have only been passive objects of male politics, can take their fate into their own hands. How can they ever become an active force if they refuse to exercise power and continue to accept the roles traditionally assigned to women?

This stereotype teaches us as women not only to refuse to take up arms but also to refuse to interfere in the planning of those who use and design weapons and buy and sell them. As usual, no women participated in the SALT II disarmament talks.

The question remains, of course, whether things would be any different if women did participate in disarmament conferences. Is the army an appropriate institution for promoting the interests of women and of disarmament? The truth of the matter is, no doubt, in both economic and psychological terms, that women are a useful resource now because they are both cheaper and more willing workers.

At the moment, a third of our annual budget of about 59 billion marks is spent on the military establishment, and the phrase "militarization of society" has to be understood in this context. There is simply no question about it: a society that uses its resources this way is militarized. A country that has the largest military and police forces in Europe is a militarized country, at least in the eyes of its neighbors. What is new about obligatory military duty for women and what will be accelerated considerably by it is the militarization of the popular mind that will accompany it. This entire discussion promotes psychological preparation for combat readiness and for maintaining our present political priorities.

The old slogan "guns instead of butter," translated into today's terms, reads "war preparation instead of quality of life." In the coming decades, economic problems and the development of alternative sources of energy will require all the financial and intellectual reserves we have. Every mark and every mind that we waste in perpetuating our stone-age international relationships will be lost for solving the central human problems of our time. That women should be militarized in this of all moments when the threat of nuclear holocaust is hanging over us strikes me as a bad joke.

I cannot go along with those women who think they are doing something for the cause of equality by favoring military service for women. What kind of training would young girls get in the military? Should young women, too, be exposed to the demoralizing influences of boredom, alcoholism, and petty crime in this so-called school of the nation? Is this not too high a price to pay, even if some women should get the benefits of better technical training? And will the military, that most masculine of institutions, all of a sudden open its middle ranks, much less its higher ones, to women?

The major problem here seems to me to be a lack of clarity on what emancipation for women really means. There are two possible answers today to the question of what it is that women really want. Some women answer that they want their fair share of what there is to be had, whether that means money, power, opportunities, or jobs. The pie should be divided equally. This early feminist position seems remarkably blind, however, to the question of what the pie in our society actually consists of. Are we hoping, as American feminists like to ask ironically, to become vice-presidents of General Motors? Do we really want to learn the things that men in our society do: to tyrannize, command, exploit, destroy the earth?

There is another vision of women's liberation that does not assume that we want to have and do everything that men have and do. This vision does not ask for a fair share of what men already have; it asks for something altogether different. The debate over equal rights and equal opportunities overlooks to what ends these rights and opportunities are used in present-day society. The women's movement displays its real strength when it presents a vision of life that differs from the prevailing one. Women will become strong when they stop worshiping the golden calves that men worship: unlimited economic growth, national security, the balance of terror. It does not make me a freer person if I can become a soldier and thus make my contribution to the militarization of society. We shall become free only when we beat our swords into plowshares, as Isaiah says (Isa. 2:4), and when we learn to operate irrigation systems, not tanks. We shall be free and we shall be women only when we join forces with life against production for death and the ongoing preparation for murder. We shall not become free by retiring into the private sphere and saying "Count me out," nor shall we become free by conforming to a society that holds its generals and millionaires in particularly high regard.

We shall become free when we learn to work for peace actively, deliberately, and militantly.

Despair of the so-called subjective element

Three days ago
that old bore panic moved in with me again
now I have to have breakfast with her first thing in the morning
sit still and listen to her say the same things over and over again

She plays havoc with all the papers on my desk
I can't find anything anymore I sigh
hardly realizing how true it is that we
can't find anything against the overkill

I've already forgotten
to wait for your letters
my heart pounding
without dreams I'm going to the dogs
and do
what has to be done but never enough

She blots out the colors of the sky
and scornfully takes the bible out of my hand
you know all that she says
as though we were talking of marital duties
read the defense experts she says
or you won't have anything useful to say
about security

But I don't want to I say
when she finally nods off
if I stay alone just watch
she'll move in with me for good
and hand me over to them
and make me secure for the rest of my life
building bomb after bomb after bomb

The kingdom of god or the great consensus

Living in a new city
I feel the lack of friends

I lack friends who hate the things I hate
now pop bottles have been declared passive weapons
and sympathy is treated as if it were cancer
but hatred
the minimal consensus
is not enough to live by
it suffices only for dying

I lack friends who fear the things I fear
now production for internal security outstrips everything else
and the police budget will increase a third by eighty-one
but fear
the everyday consensus
between me and the baker's wife next door
is not enough for fighting
it suffices only for business as usual

Most of all I lack friends who wish the things I wish for
I read of women who dream of beating or being beaten
have those with other wishes been made voiceless
the vision
the great consensus
is still a long way off
swords are still not plowshares
tanks still not tractors
money spent on security creates no jobs
the blind are not allowed to see for themselves
the kingdom of god the great consensus
is right here in our midst
promised a long time ago

Living in a new city
I lack friends
to help me believe

Play me a song about rosa, anna, and rosa

Leave me alone with your identity crises
stop your introspective strumming on the guitar
play something else
play a song about peace
play about our comrades in the struggle

Sing about anna walentinowić
crane operator in danzig
sing of the strike and why it broke out
and don't forget rosa parks
don't ever forget that she stayed seated
for each one of us no matter how white our skin
stayed seated in the bus in alabama
where blacks were not supposed to sit

Sing about women
just looking at them makes me stronger
makes me laugh
solidly built like anna the crane operator
who scared them so much they fired her to avoid trouble
a preventive layoff from her job on the crane

Don't forget our great sister rosa luxemburg either
she came from anna's country
that small country thirsting for freedom
split and gagged occupied and possessed
beaten and raped
but never subdued
sing about rosa
and about the spontaneity of the people
she believed in
like anna the crane operator

Did you see her picture
sing another song about anna
about the hope of the dock workers
for meat and the right to defend themselves
for bread and for roses

Anna walentinowić
the papers don't carry your story
because people here don't know
what it means to be a woman
a human being
a crane operator
who makes strikes possible
because we're still expected to admire sweet little bunnies
not a woman with a laugh like anna's
with four children and now and then
a preventive layoff

Stop your introspective strumming on the guitar
play something else
play a song about peace
play about comrades in the struggle

I'm tired of all this whining
play me a song about anna and the two rosas
play about real people
about women strong and vulnerable
caring for others and independent
fighting for you too in the teller's cage at Chase Manhattan bank
for all our sisters
play about bread and roses
play about the price of meat and a free labor union
play against steel helmets and what's inside them
play against atomic missiles and what's behind them
you can't arrest the sun
                              it shines
you can't censor the roses
                              they flower
you can't keep women down
                              they laugh

Play about rosa luxemburg
play about rosa parks
play about anna walentinowić
play about our sisters
play about us

We Say No!

Dear Women and Men for Peace,

I want to tell you my fears; I want to tell you my hopes.

My fears have grown since December 1979 when NATO decided to increase the nuclear weaponry stationed in Europe. I regard that decision as a major historical event, far more important, say, than the Soviet invasion of Afghanistan. Future generations may look back and speak of the period before December 1979 as the period after World War II. And they may call the period after December 1979 the period before World War III.

Our country is being militarized through and through. Recruits are sworn into the army with great pomp and circumstance and extensive publicity. All of a sudden our poor generals in the army have discovered that they do not have any medals to wear, and they are experiencing an altogether new need to decorate themselves. The defense budget is increased and funding for everything else—schools, health care, the creation of jobs—is cut. And now the slogan "women in the army" is being bandied about and even represented as a step forward in the cause of women's liberation. A state that is becoming increasingly incapable of offering young women meaningful education is now guaranteeing them everything if they put on the uniform: useful training, steady jobs, equal opportunity. We want and need those things but not at the hands of the military. We want them as normal and nonmilitary rights for all women in our country.

Women in the military is only one facet of a general militarization. War is being made to appear thinkable again. We have to plan for our defense, so called. The arms buildup is represented as a catching-up exercise. But there is only one thing to be said about those 572 medium-range missiles that NATO wants to station in Europe: they are 572 too many. We do not need them. They do not make us more secure; they only make utterly clear that nothing will be left of us if they are ever used. Military experts with common sense have even admitted that. We have to prevent the NATO decision from being translated into reality.

Our demands are: No women in the military! No more nuclear missiles in western Europe!

I am encouraged by the growing peace movement in our country. There is a goodly number of us here right now, and that number is growing every day. I have learned a lot from our peacemaking friends in Holland. The antimilitaristic movement is so strong there that a minister can threaten to resign if any more atomic bombs are stationed in Holland. One of the slogans of the Dutch is: "Free the world of atomic weapons. Start in the Netherlands." "Let's clear the Netherlands first" is another. A time will come when we shall be ready to say that for West Germany too.

When I first heard about the Dutch reaction, I asked myself why it is that one war was quite enough for the Dutch, whereas for us Germans not even two are enough. In our country, there are still people who have not learned much—and certainly not enough—even from two wars. There are still people here who feel compelled to get ready for a third war. The more militarism and the more atomic bombs we have, the safer they feel. But their number is shrinking. Even government ministers know that, and that is why they are asking for military studies in the schools, and that is why they are making all sorts of promises to lure women into voluntary service. But we cannot be bought, and we cannot be sold down the river either. We say no, loud and clear. We defend ourselves. We resist. We will not go along with the tide one more time. We have had enough! If every man and woman here can convince—let us say—twelve friends to fight for peace and not let the powers that be do as they will with them, then we shall really be getting somewhere. Twelve more for every one here: then we shall really be getting somewhere.

Indigestion on the increase

One bottle of coke contains more sugar
than my grandmother consumed in a month
    the oversaturation we suffer is promoted
    to transform our hunger for food
    into an addiction for the unusual
neither hungry nor full
I eat something for the sake of eating

One daily newspaper contains more half-lies
than my grandmother was exposed to in a month
    the oversaturation with misery
    we can do nothing about
    is promoted to transform our hunger for justice
    into an addiction for the unusual
neither sad nor happy
I read something for the sake of reading

One half-hour of a morning tv show contains more vapid talk
than my grandmother listened to in a month
    the oversaturation with a language that conveys nothing
    is promoted to eradicate sympathy
    and to make our desire to touch others with words
    appear ridiculous
neither seriously nor playfully
I talk for the sake of talking

To become a human being in these times
is about as likely
as for a camel
to pass through the eye of a needle

Five hundred seventy-two

Some dutch citizens will withhold
five guldens and seventy-two cents from the state
that plans to station
five hundred and seventy-two medium-range atomic missiles
in europe

This symbolic amount of tax resistance
seems to me ridiculously insignificant
but in my country
where the imagination is underdeveloped
in the free democratic social order I live in
where there is no right to resist
among my people
where goliath is honored and david unheard of

This amount makes me cry rather than laugh

When I was asked for the 572nd time what I thought about violence

My pacifist friends
proceeded with extreme violence
at an innocent general electric plant
located in a peaceloving town
named king of prussia
when they used an instrument of violence
the old-fashioned hammer
to render some harmless instruments of security
namely atomic missiles useless

To justify their irresponsible action
they quoted a man
from the eighth century bc
whose followers they appeared to be
and who was apparently possessed by the crazy idea
of beating swords into plowshares
on behalf of a higher being

And in the interest of lower beings
people too lazy to work and fringe groups
this violent coalition
of the very high and the very low
of what they call god and what they call the poor
represents for us in the neutral middle
a genuine threat to security

Our Numbers Are Growing Every Day

Hamburg, January 1981

Dear Sisters,

I am sorry that I will not be in Germany on March 8, 1981, for the women's congress, but I will be very much with you in my thoughts and in my heart, and I hope that the spirit that comforts and lends courage will be with you, the spirit that we in the Christian tradition call the Holy Spirit.

It is a comfort to me that our numbers are growing every day. The situation is too serious for us to be able to relegate it to the men in power. Our medium-range goal should be to bring the Federal Republic to the point that Holland has reached. Following the example of the Dutch, we should try to win about half of our population and half of our parliament over to the cause of peace. "Free the world of atomic weapons. Start in the Federal Republic."

I am consoled by every young man who responds to the nuclear arms buildup by refusing to serve in the German army—an army that does not defend us anymore but makes us, with its first-strike weapons, the first target that would be attacked in an atomic war. I am consoled by every young woman who rejects the caresses of hands that are learning to kill. I am consoled by every working man and woman who asks what purpose his or her production serves, by every scientist who reflects on the uses to which his or her research is put. I am consoled above all by every man in the street and every housewife who will not just "go along" and be obedient for the third time in this century. Anyone who keeps silent and plays dead is already dead.

The Spirit that guides our actions not only consoles; the Spirit

Fear not

Those in power can no longer overlook the handwriting on the wall
their subjects think twice about nodding in agreement
the weapons dealers no longer dare to walk all over the weak
bishops stop equivocating and say no
the friends of jesus block the roads of overkill
school children learn the truth

How are we to recognize an angel
except that he brings courage where fear was
joy where even sadness refused to grow
objections where hard facts used to rule the day
disarmament where terror was a credible deterrent

Fear not resistance is growing

also gives us courage. It is not true that we women are too ignorant and lack the expertise to understand the truth. Human beings are capable of dealing with the truth, and we have to make the simple truth unmistakably clear to the present government.

The truth is that every one of the 112 cruise missiles destined to be stationed in the territory of the Federal Republic carries a warhead with ten times the destructive power of the bomb dropped on Hiroshima.

The truth is that atomic weapons are targets for other atomic weapons.

The truth is that madness of this kind can be imposed on a population only in a military dictatorship that exploits the ideology of "security" to dispense with all democratic rights (the right to publish, to strike, to demonstrate). We women are to be made subject to military service too, and so be made accomplices to murder.

But the Spirit gives us courage to recognize the truth, to gather the information we need, and to propagate the truth. If the media refuse to help us, we will be the medium ourselves. Whenever we act fearlessly, we become the epistle of Christ that everyone can read (see 2 Cor. 3:3).

The courage that the Holy Spirit gives us spurs our imaginations too. We shall devise new methods for the struggle, methods learned from such pioneers of nonviolence as Gandhi, Martin Luther King, Jr., and the Bolivian women who freed fifty-two political prisoners by their hunger strike. Like these people, we shall openly initiate illegal actions. It is no disgrace to go to prison for peace, but it is a disgrace to let the powerful do as they will with us. The atomic arming of Europe under the leadership of the West German government is an act of war. No one asked us whether we wanted a total arms buildup. Even the government knows that Germans who have learned something from history will not say yes to war again.

It violates human dignity to let oneself be pushed around and manipulated. We are capable of grasping the truth; we are capable of making peace, even if we are told day after day that we are not.

In the Spirit that consoles and lends courage, we say no to:

- those who are planning atomic war
- those who are preparing atomic war
- those who are profiting from atomic war.

75

You can say yes only if you have learned to say no. Women the world over are spelling out a new yes, for themselves, for their children, for the poor and the wives of the poor, who are the poorest of the poor. For peace. Let us join them.

Answer to the question, whether christianity has a liberating effect on me

Church was always boring
I hear people say but
the woman who tells me this
has long since given up on life

It didn't speak to me
I hear people say but
I didn't hear anyone speaking
once the loudspeaker was turned off

It always scared me
I hear people say but
the man who tells me this works every day
to improve the methods of overkill

The gospel taught me to cry
it made me scared of those without fears
it spoke to me among those without speech
it made me thirsty among those who are bored

That is relative progress

The process of remembering

Once this summer
a cuckoo kept calling and calling*
I rack my brain trying to remember
when it was and why
a wild joy came over me
once this summer

I can see the hillside with the grass gone to seed
the grown-up children leaning against a bench
my nose starts to itch with hay fever
the clouds collect again
once this summer
a cuckoo kept calling and calling

My wild joy in counting
as if he were impossible to eradicate
or to drive away
once in this summer
of preparations for world war three
a cuckoo kept calling and calling

*Note: according to German folklore the number of times a cuckoo calls is supposed
to foretell how many more years a person will live.

The happiness of being alive

But what compels you to leave
the mystical golden green tree
and why do you have to see it in the context
of the pershing two missiles
and their improved accuracy

Ah but can't you understand
happiness more than I can hold
fear more than I can breathe
my happiness makes me grow
so that I can't live for myself alone

It's no effort and no obligation
nor is it a hobby for after-work hours
it's simply the happiness of being alive
that makes me declare peace over and over again
to those who live under the ogre's thumb

States of depression

Someone told me about a woman who
in a state of deep depression
like you perhaps who are reading this
abandoned by the man
she had thought of as hers for a time
as I did years ago
and later not having learned any better
went to the photocopy machine with some poems
like the one you are reading now
made copies and sent them to friends
hear me my younger sister
for whom I write more than for anyone else
they say she did that again and again
before she killed herself

Someone told me that story
because there's a point she said
in writing poems
I honestly don't know

To accompany someone
whom we leave alone in the end

To carry a message around
that I can't deliver

Not to the woman I didn't know
nor to those I know all too well
the advocates of stockpiling death
can I convey

What it means
to love god above all else

Letter to a Friend

January 1980

Dear Ruth,

Every morning the Indian mothers ask their children what they dreamed, the way we ask our children how things were in school today. To dream one's dream and to communicate it—that's a very important thing. I'd like to put my questions to you in this spirit, and this is how I'd like to be questioned myself.

Freimut Duve asked a number of writers about their vision of a "republic of the peaceloving," and I thought it would be useful to talk with you about this. Then I read your paper, and what you had to say made me feel confused, what you said about powerlessness, about the powerlessness of the blacks in South Africa who don't fight back, about the powerlessness of women who have resigned themselves to being colonized. You said, in agreement with black theology, that it is a sin to live without power, that it is a negation of what we were created for, which is to be the image of God and to share in his power to create life, to make life possible, and to liberate it.

I wanted to send you my ideas on a humane republic of the peaceful, but now I'm hesitating. Can I talk about the meek who will inherit the earth in the midst of the preparations for a third world war that are going on around us now? The sin you spoke of gets in my way. I'm overcome by a feeling of absolute powerlessness. I could immolate myself and it wouldn't do the least bit of good. I have no connection with the power to make peace. I stand apart from life, from God, if you will. Sin—i.e., accepting the impotence we feel—is no theological fairy tale but the most real and urgent problem we have to deal with every day, an onerous day-by-day chore.

Can we even envision a "republic of peacemakers" in a society that we see turning more and more militaristic? Doesn't it amount to overestimating the power of our dreams and underestimating the power of the sin that tells us there's absolutely nothing we can do? I feel every bit as helpless as a black schoolgirl in Soweto. I do not feel any less at the mercy of violence and terror. The violence I mean is state-instigated violence, and the terror is industrial terror. How, given this militarization of society, do we combat powerlessness?

In recent months I have sometimes felt like a rabbit paralyzed by its fright of a snake. Now, I felt, a phase in the military history of our country is coming to an end. The old ideas—that NATO existed to spring to the defense if any member country were attacked, that pacifism is better than militarism—are being swept away. More and more hawks are speaking out; the arms race is being escalated; the military budget has been increased; private companies are advertising bombproof cellars; students fantasize about emigrating to Australia. Let's build up our weaponry, we heard a few weeks ago; there'll be time to negotiate later.

The Russian invasion of Afghanistan couldn't have come at a more opportune time. It justified in retrospect the argument that we should build up our arms so that we could disarm later. But wasn't it the NATO decision of December 12, 1979, that made this invasion possible? For only after this disappointment could the hawks in Moscow win the upper hand. Only isolated voices spoke for the reverse order—i.e., that we start by negotiating and then, under conditions that might be different, reconsider whether we needed to continue to arm. What will the arms race look like in the year 2000?

No one who is advocating a preventive arms buildup now can seriously believe that it will be possible later, by means of negotiation, to turn the arms-race calendar back. I do not know of any instance in military history when a planning staff, a military unit, or even an economic lobby that once had a bomb contract in its pocket ever let its new toy be taken away from it. I can't imagine anything less likely from either a psychological or economic point of view. It frightens me how we passively accept the fact that tanks are ruining our highways, that natural sanctuaries are being taken

Combatting sadness

I'll tell you all my strategies
I put on my shirt with the seven clasps
because aside from killing I like being a soldier
then I drink a lot of hot coffee
because being cold seems to me a kind of irresoluteness
then I straighten up the papers on my desk
decide to dispose of some throw them out and learn to say no
then I think of those even more defenseless than I
and less well equipped

In view of the fact that none of these strategies
will necessarily lead to victory
I reflect on the difference between a battle and a war
I remain dependent and am defeated time and again

Finally I ask you what methods you use
to combat sadness
and live

over for military maneuvers, that the military can "educate" our young, that increased military spending is weakening our educational and social institutions.

Not long ago the defense lobby initiated discussion on when women could finally join the German army. From the outset, the question was not whether but when. That is only logical: a military, technological escalation requires psychological preparation. Brains have to be washed. Expectations are raised with talk of educational opportunities for girls who have a technical bent but can't find any openings in our economy. A willingness to serve in the military is created with the help of discussions like these that consider—with utter objectivity, of course—the pros and cons of the issue.

During those weeks when the public mind in our country was becoming more and more militarized, I tried to ward off the sin of powerlessness, of sheer despair, and develop some sense of hope. What would a republic of peacemakers, a country in search of peace, look like? How could the occupied territory that more and more people feel this country is becoming turn into a country for human beings?

I want to try to keep my dream within the limits of the possible. Strange as this may sound, I still have not given up my vision of a *church of the peaceloving.* I'd like to talk to you and many others about this. I have some concrete experiences to go on, and I also have echoing in my ear the promises that the prophets held out long ago to the people of Israel and to all humankind, the promise of a gentle, a peaceful land. A church of peacemakers, a church of peace, would be a first step toward that goal and an aid in achieving it.

I am not talking about any thing like "the Christmas spirit" here. I am talking about ordinary pacifists, militant peaceniks who say no to killing in any form. No to plans for killing or to portraying other countries as our enemies. No to training to kill and to learning to take aim at other human beings. No to research that serves the cause of death (in the United States today 51 percent of all scientists are involved in war-related projects and serve the great death machine). No to the financing of the capability to kill. I dream of a militant no: refusal, sabotage, resistance. That is what a church of the peaceful would stand for. A church of peacemakers would not be able to give its blessing to weapons or to those who

A sort of love poem

A few more like you bob
not at all extreme
or drunk with expectations
but still armed
with the normal love for peace
they try to wean us from and order us to shed
bit by bit
to get us ready for their war
against the migratory birds

Of these you speak in a tone
not at all extreme
more like a new englander
but still with eyes
for the normal flyways of the birds
eyes they are trying to blind
if need be with gas

A few more like you bob
a few more like your friends
let's say a million more
and we could declare peace
on those who abolish it
turning brute force
against the migratory birds

want to bear arms. As long as we have not beaten swords into plowshares and as long as we have not made tractors and school buses out of medium-range missiles, it would be the task of this church to help put the death machine out of commission—illegally but nonviolently.

A church of the peaceful could perhaps study and teach theology in the underground but not at the military academies of the *Bundeswehr*. Theology would arise wherever people assumed responsibility for illegal actions in the name of peace and were willing to go to jail for the sake of peace, speaking out that clear no to militarism that we need to hear. Everyone confirmed in this church, as I picture it, would understand the connection between militarism and mass poverty in the Third World, and everyone would understand their own part in perpetuating that connection.

"All who draw the sword will die by the sword" (Matt. 26:52). Why is that not inscribed on the walls of churches, even though it does not appear on the walls of military installations?

The status quo in the world, the international division of labor between us, the rich, the exporters of technology, and the areas with the lowest wages and the cheapest labor has to be perpetuated by military force. The impoverishment of countries in which it does not pay to invest, because, unlike South Africa, Brazil, or Gabun, they do not have dictators who will guarantee order and profits, is deliberately planned. The Trilateral Commission's ideas on preserving the existing balance of economic power demonstrate this. The form of injustice in which we live has to be defended by force; the apartheid we support, with our technology and our trade, has to be kept secure. Our standard of living makes wars of conquest a necessity. That became clear in the most recent statements of the CDU's military expert, Wörner.

Property and militarization, markets and weapons, go hand in hand today more than ever before. When Francis of Assisi was asked eight centuries ago if a life without property wasn't hard and overly burdensome, he replied: "If we want to own things, we also have to have weapons to defend ourselves. This is where all the quarrels and battles that make love impossible come from. And this is why we do not want to own anything." A church of the peaceful would be a church in the spirit of St. Francis.

We must not say or even think in a remote corner of our hearts that these are foolish utopian thoughts. We must not let militarism destroy our dreams and desires too, forcing the sin of powerlessness on us. I want to make clear to you, Ruth, and to your friends and to everyone who is in danger of opting out either by inner resignation or by emigration or by trying to live some bucolic idyll, that Christians have overcome the sin of powerlessness in the past. There have been Christians who did not subordinate their Christianity to the joint authority of throne and altar. There have been churches of peacemakers in the past, churches of peace. There have been Christians who have not worn the inscription "God with us" on the buckle of their field packs but have written it on their tax forms when they refused to pay war taxes.

I can think of two important examples in the recent past. The first is the resistance of American Christians to the Vietnam war, resistance that helped put an end to the genocide in Southeast Asia—militant, illegal resistance. Christians publicly poured napalm on draft cards and burned them. For weeks at a time they blocked trains carrying war material by sitting on the tracks. Many of my friends in the United States say as a matter of course about certain periods during those years, "Oh, I was in jail then."

The other example is the resistance of the Dutch to so-called arms equalization, resistance in which Christians have played a major role. As the *Frankfurter Rundschau* put it, "No church support, no missiles." The Dutch parliament voted against the stationing of medium-range missiles in Holland. That was a sign of peace. In Utrecht alone twenty thousand people demonstrated under the slogan "Disarmament negotiations, yes—modernization, no." This decision the Dutch made would not have been conceivable without the years of patient peace education the churches did to prepare the way for it. It would not have been possible without the Interdenominational Peace Council either, for which there is no comparable organization in our much wealthier German churches.

Just across the border, then, we can see the beginnings of a rainbow between God and an earth no longer cursed.

Is it utopian to imagine a church that would suffer more from increases in the defense budget than from legalized abortion? In a country whose entire Christian tradition has been formed by respect for authority, the idea of an antimilitaristic church sounds like a mockery. Whenever I mention Christian anarchism here, my audience looks at me as if I were from the moon.

But taking the Sermon on the Mount seriously is not anywhere near as remote a thing as the moon. "Happy the gentle," it says, for "they shall have the earth for their heritage" (Matt. 5:3). A church of peace, a church of the people, a church of the gentle that gathers grassroots power from below to pit against the power from above, a church like that could be a genuine oppositional force in a society that is not gentle at all and that is becoming increasingly militaristic.

Should not the fact that the Dutch Christian Democrats have adopted the rejection of nuclear weapons as part of their program prompt the hawks in our CDU to rethink their position? Should not at least an inquiry be possible, a dialogue, an alternative in our lifestyle and in our political expectations?

Even in our country of the ungentle there are groups of Christians willing to live without the protection of weapons. Perhaps someday they will rediscover the militancy of faith, militancy against the godless powerlessness that those colonialized by militarism feel.

So keep on praying and resisting, as always. St. Francis lives! Don't ever forget that.

Your sister,
Dorothee Sölle

The young man with the unruly red hair

When the young man with the unruly red hair stood up
how could he possibly explain to the leaders of his party
when he refused to be satisfied with glib answers
and asked in his working-class accent
how I expected to explain to my old aunt in germany
the infamous spd*

What Christ means
that's literally what the redhead said
and why the only thing feasible is death
is death is death he started to stammer
and when he started for the third time
to ask a nonacademic question
in a british college

I finally paid attention and realized
that this was a cry
I finally looked and discovered
the wings on his shabby raincoat
god always has I thought
ordered his angels over us
so that we don't have to die
of the loneliness of those who fight

*Social Democratic Party

A child's questions

There's much to fear my little one
that I can't do anything about
grandmother died
and they need tanks for war

There's much I can't do anything about
when you ask my little one
grandmother used to peel potato ribbons
and peace is an itsy-bitsy millet grain

The big boys driving the tanks
are afraid too and would rather not
the kingdom of god is even tinier
than you were and will be a tree
for us to live under

God Lives Unprotected

I want to begin this meditation on the day of Christ's death with my recollections of a religious service I took part in last year.

A small group of Christians, among them a few Catholic nuns and a large number of Spanish-speaking refugees, stood in front of the White House in Washington. The sun had come out; tourists were streaming by. Occasionally one would stop for a while or join us. We had chosen as our theme an old symbol of Christian piety, the contemplation of the Stations of the Cross. Jesus is taken captive, he is interrogated, he is crowned with thorns, he collapses for the first time under the weight of the cross, and so on, until his death by torture. A speaker reminded us that this was the day of Christ's death, that on this same day eleven years earlier Martin Luther King, Jr., was shot, and that a few weeks ago Oscar Romero, the archbishop of San Salvador, was murdered as he was celebrating mass.

As the different stations of Christ's suffering were named, large placards illustrating the life of the people in El Salvador today were held up. For the text "He is taken prisoner" a photograph showing the *Guardia Civil*, the police, shoving peasants into a jeep was shown. Passers-by and those of us taking part in the service saw women searching in a village for their young sons who had been abducted and probably murdered. For the text "He collapses for the first time under the weight of the cross," we saw a body riddled with bullets lying by the roadside. Under the inscription "He is whipped," we saw modern instruments of torture, among them the *picana*—an electrical torture device—and the water bucket in which the victim's head is held until he almost drowns.

The commentary was brief and sober. We prayed together, mostly traditional prayers. A photograph of Oscar Romero lay on the grass. An allusion was made to Pontius Pilate, who sits in the White House and washes his hands because he allegedly has nothing to do with all this. There was reflection, shock, pain. There were the agitated faces of the young refugees from Uruguay, Chile, Argentina, who had had experiences like these or just barely escaped having them. We were a small group, forty at the most. Thousands of busy workers and tourists passed by.

Later, in keeping with my own German traditions, I went to one of those immense neo-Gothic cathedrals to hear a concert of religious music. I sat among people who were better dressed than the group in front of the White House. I listened to baroque music in an atmosphere that I felt to be unthinking and devoid of emotion.

These two experiences of Good Friday were worlds apart, but at the end of that day I knew quite clearly where I belonged: on the street, not in the solemn church with its thin music, not under the shadow of the organ's tones. I belonged with that unrespected group that was not enjoying Good Friday esthetically but making the connections between it and present-day suffering. This is what it must have been like for the first Christians, I thought: a fringe group of outsiders, looked down upon by others, out of place in the official cults that were all devoted to sanctioning the power of the state, to glorifying the marvelous lives of the high and mighty, to keeping quiet about the oppressed lives of the masses. Today, those masses make up two-thirds of the world's population, and they are condemned to the same poverty and hunger now as they were then. I use the biblical designation for them: "the poor."

I think we can understand Christ's death only if we see the torture and execution that he suffered (and that we euphemize by calling the "passion") in the light of what is happening today. We can understand it only if we share in the battle to the death and in the pain that people are forced to suffer today in the name of justice.

It is not a matter of indifference whether or not we make this connection between Christ and the present-day situation. If we fail to make it, we are simply denying Jesus. We have to "draw him into our flesh," as Luther put it, into our historical flesh, into what is significant to people today. When Luther used this expression, his meaning was a clearly polemical one. It is aimed at those who do not want to draw Christ into their concrete, everyday flesh but want to spiritualize him so that he has nothing to do with

Three facts from the biography of the new secretary of state

Well-versed in service
haig saw to it that 18½ minutes of richard nixon's tapes
disappeared for good
and nixon went free a respected man

Tested in loyalty
the nixon protégé could not be given supreme command
without confirmation from the senators in washington
so he bypassed democratic rigamarole on his way to brussels

At home in business
al haig was is and will remain president of
united technology
the biggest supplier of weapons
on earth at this time

Well-versed in the service of the ogre
tested in loyalty to him
at home in the business of gobbling people up
he assumes his office

campesinos being tortured to death in El Salvador. To draw him into the flesh means to bring him out of abstraction, out of the distance, out of mere intellectual preoccupation into the reality we have to live with.

He concerned himself with political reality, even then. Jesus gave his own life because he loved the poor. Had he loved the rich above all and only them, as we like to assume for utterly transparent reasons, then he would not have had to die. The great confrontation at the end of his life, the one that took him to Jerusalem where the powers that be had their stronghold, makes sense only if we see it as a confrontation in the interest of the poor. Jesus' political base, his following, was stronger in Galilee. There he could heal the sick, feed the hungry, and spread his message. But the real illness afflicting the people was located elsewhere; if they were truly going to satisfy their hunger, they needed a far more radical redistribution of the goods of this earth. Words alone were apparently not enough to make his message comprehensible.

Jesus is a man who gave his life for love of the poor. He gave his life away instead of hoarding it and making it secure. He threw it away, or so his family thought, and they also thought he was more or less mad. What they were right about was that he did what he did of his own free will.

There was no compulsion, in the sense that God had created Jesus to suffer and now he was obliged to do what was preordained for him. That is bad theology: it overlooks the element of freedom. We might say that God had created Jesus to love—that is, created him for the greatest freedom imaginable. And this love led, as every serious love does, to suffering. It led Jesus to the center of power, to Jerusalem. From the provinces to the capital, from the rural synagogue to the temple, from the poor to the rich. It led him from obscurity to visibility.

A political song from Chile says that to love means not to hide your face. Jesus hid his face less and less. In the end, what he was became completely visible. They tortured him so long that there was nothing opaque, nothing partial, nothing cautious, nothing reserved left in him. Then he could say: it is accomplished. Here I am, a human being for others.

A new quality of human existence had been achieved, something for which there were no words in the language of that time. Jesus' secret, his power, his refusal to hide his face, had to be given some kind of name. The expression that Jesus' first friends found and that, in their opinion, came closest to expressing what they meant was "Son of God," "Son of the Highest." How could anyone give that name to a political criminal who had just been tortured to death? A Roman centurion stood by the cross on Good Friday and "saw" who this Jesus was. "Truly this man was the son of God." What did he mean by that? What I think he meant was: this man did not hide his face. This man gave his life because he loved the poor. This man was as near to God as a son is to his father. He has made visible the truth we have done nothing but talk about. He was the truth: light, water, the bread of life. This, at any rate, is what his followers meant when they called him God's son.

Jesus lived without protection. That is not a statement of faith but a simple statement of fact. He renounced the protection that a family can offer. He did not want the protection that property can give. He chose to keep silent rather than make use of the protection his eloquence could have given him. He explicitly rejected the protection that weapons and armies can provide. When Peter tried to defend him when he was taken captive, he said: "Put your sword back, for all who draw the sword will die by the sword. Or do you think that I cannot appeal to my Father who would promptly send more than twelve legions of angels to my defense?" (Matt. 26:52–53). In the Roman army, a legion usually consisted of six thousand men. The term is used here to stand symbolically for an infinitely large number. If Jesus had wanted protection, he could have asked God for it and let God protect him. But he does not ask God for protection. He lives and acts without protection. The officials in power treat him like a dangerous criminal who is likely to resist with violence, but he could have been captured easily in broad daylight in the temple where he taught without protection and without giving a thought to fleeing. "It was at this time that Jesus said to the crowds, 'Am I a brigand, that you had to set out to capture me with swords and clubs? I sat teaching in the Temple day after day and you never laid hands on me' " (Matt. 26:55–56).

Jesus lived without protection. When his vulnerability became visible, when he rejected the natural response of striking back when attacked, when he refused to hope for the intervention of a higher power, at that point his disciples left him and fled. They apparently could not tolerate vulnerability; if that was the only alternative, they preferred violence; they preferred to be armed; at the very least they preferred to be able to make threats.

But Jesus lived without protection. He did not just put up with his vulnerability; he chose it voluntarily. He chose to live without weapons, without violence, and without the protection that force—even if only in the form of threats—can offer. Jesus was not armed, and he did not seek out the arms of others to hide behind. This kind of vulnerability has a provocative effect.

This is the very effect that Jesus' disciples came to feel. And this is why they began one day to call this man who had lived nonviolently among them, without protection and without weapons, the "Son of God." This was an affirmation of Jesus' way of living without weapons. "He is the Son of God" did not mean: he has at his disposal all the weapons, all the legions, all the threats, all that he needs to destroy an enemy. It means just the opposite of "God with us" on the field-pack buckles of any army.

Jesus' vulnerability, his renunciation of violence as the core of our perception of him as the son, friend, heir, manifestor, realizer of God implies an understanding of God different from the one generally accepted today. If the disciples were right when they called him the "Son of God" and if this expression reveals an essential truth, then the word "God" must have a meaning totally different from the one we usually give it.

If Jesus is the one who does not hide his face, then God cannot very well continue to hide his either. If Jesus lives and acts nonviolently, then God too will have to manage without violence. If Jesus became free of fear, then God too has to become free of fear—which is to say, he will have to renounce force of arms. It is customary in our society—whether we believe in God or not—to worship power, to honor strength, to favor the use of force, especially when force takes the form of violence perpetrated by the state and the police. We are much more subject to the spell of violence than we suspect. To live means to live without protection, not to hide. But we hide our faces from those who are starving; and we show them instead the legions of destruction we hold at the ready.

As more and more people came to see the nonviolent and unprotected man from Nazareth as the Son of God and began to call him the Son of God, the understanding of God changed. John expressed this by saying that Jesus makes the invisible God known or interprets him. The operative word here is "exegesis"; Jesus is the exegesis of God. "No one has ever seen God; it is the only Son, who is nearest to the Father's heart, who has made him known" (John 1:18). Christ makes visible the God that we want to see but cannot see, makes him visible so that we can know anew who God is and where we can search for him. Christ interprets God to be love that gives itself freely.

God does not want to protect himself or keep himself remote. God renounced violence and the kind of intervention that those in power practice. God does not make use of violence. In Jesus Christ, God disarmed himself. God surrendered himself without protection and without arms to those who keep crying for more and more protection and arms. In Jesus Christ, God renounced violence. And of course he did this unilaterally, without waiting for us to lay down our weapons first. In Christ, God disarmed unilaterally. He took the first step. He did not wait for others, insisting that they be the first to lay down their weapons. In Christ, he began unilaterally, on his own side, to renounce the threat of violence.

Not long ago on television I saw a leader of the Protestant Church speak on the question: "Arms Buildup or Disarmament: Where Does the Church Stand?" He spoke primarily about military requirements, and when the reporter interviewing him pressed him for a theological perspective, he responded that from a theological point of view we are all guilty before God. He said, as I recall, that we are all guilty whether we possess weapons or not. The first thing that came to his mind theologically was guilt. When Protestant church leaders stress above all else in disarmament debates that we are all sinners, what they are doing is denying the existence of a God who refuses to make threats and rejects the use of violence.

If the most essential element of Christian faith is sin and not our capacity for love, if the first thing that should come to our minds in church and in our religious life is our impotence, our weakness, our guilt, our repeated failures, then the die is already cast. Then we cultivate our own fears and coddle our own need for security. We deny that human beings are capable of making peace; we abandon the unarmed Christ and run away just as the disciples did when Jesus was taken captive and when it became clear that protection and weapons were useless now. We are tempted to look for other masters who offer more protection and security.

The old vicious circle takes this form: we are weak and we feel weak. We are afraid and we teach others to be afraid. We seek safety—that is, we wall ourselves in and hide behind the armor plate of power, hide in the control towers of devastation, feel weak again, and therefore feel compelled to press the button.

Christ broke out of this vicious circle in which we still live, this vicious circle of weakness, fear, need for protection, need for security, need for violence. It is not true, he told us, that you are weak. You can do whatever you want if you have faith. You are strong; you are beautiful. You do not need to build any walls to hide behind. You can live without armaments. Because you are strong, you can put the neurotic need for security behind you. You do not need to defend your life like a lunatic. For love of the poor, Jesus says, you can give your life away and spread it around. The mechanism that runs its course from weakness to a need for security to violence is unsound. God is in you. You do not need to protect yourself. It is possible to live without violence and without weapons.

PART TWO

To Love Means
Not to Hide

"I have no political analysis of resistance to offer that justifies hope. We have to expect the worst, for a while. But I know from the tradition that sustains the struggling and suffering people of El Salvador that terror will not have the last word."

D.S.

Saturday before easter '81

Oh when
will the graves finally be empty
the exhuming of victims unnecessary
the pictures gone
of children sprayed with a new poison
that turns the skin black and peeling
and makes the eyes sink into their sockets
oh when
will the graves finally be empty
of mutilated bodies
in el salvador

When I first became a christian
I wanted to see christ
striking me down on the road to damascus
I pictured the place something like göttingen
the empty tomb was no more than a fairy tale
for the unenlightened

Now I've been becoming a christian
for a long time
and I have occasionally seen jesus
the last time as an old woman in nicaragua
who was learning to read she was beaming
not just her eyes but also her hair thinned by age
and her twisted feet
she was beaming all over

But I've also grown poorer
depressed I scurry through the city
I even go to demonstrations
half expecting courage to be passed out there
and I'd give anything to see
the other half of the story
the empty tomb on easter morning
and empty graves in el salvador

Chile summer '78

I can get used to the begging
sometimes I give sometimes I don't
because I'm in too big a hurry
or out of indifference
or for lack of change

It's hard getting used to
the old woman who talks incessantly
they came to get her husband five years ago
she gives me her address
nobody writes to her
because they're too busy
or out of indifference
or for lack of time

I will not get used to
the photograph of a 22-year-old
last seen at a torture center
one and a half years ago
his mother looks me in the face
and I take the picture
and carry it around with me
despite my being busy
my indifference
and my chronic lack of time
the way one carries a child
for months
the picture in my pocket

And I promise you
mother of 551054 stgo
not to get used
to the disappearing
the being left alone
the begging

for your sake
I shall not get used to anything
we shall not let ourselves be comfortable
with the coexistence of
begging and disappearances
torture and soccer
fear and profit

Girl from chile

Girl from chile
with long smooth hair
over the broad indian face
I see you put down the receiver
in the phone booth
and smile
and cross the street
and smile
and I know what you said
and to whom

Girl from chile
yesterday I saw one of your sisters
so weak she was lying on a bed
because she had eaten nothing for two weeks
because of her father
taken away disappeared tortured perhaps murdered
girl from chile
yesterday I saw your sister
smile your smile
beneath the gentle steady eyes
when she talked about her father
and about her headache
and about her father

Girl from chile
in your country
love and hunger
smiling and strikes
women and strength
go together
girl from chile
little sister
share your smile with us
your hunger for justice
your struggle
that brings out beauty

Human Rights in Latin America

On the Problem of Political Abductions

In September 1979 I met an Argentine pastor in Buenos Aires who had been a student of mine in New York. He introduced me to his sister. The police had interrogated her husband in their home on a Friday evening. Monday morning he wanted to go to work as usual. He said he had done nothing illegal or subversive. He was a Peronist, Ernesto's sister added. The daughter went to school, the son to work, the mother to her office, and the father left the house too. That was in 1977. He has not been seen again since. No trace has been found, no clue to his whereabouts.

This woman is one of the 5,580 people in Argentina who have applied for writs of habeas corpus. She numbers among the relatives of the missing. Her experience is like that of the mothers of the Plaza de Mayo who gathered every Thursday afternoon in silent protest in front of the government building in Buenos Aires, until they were forbidden to do so. She is one of those women whom government officials call *las locas*, the madwomen, who refuse to keep silent and who go underground or leave the country only in the face of the most extreme threats.

She is among those who ask that utterly simple and most human of questions that is being asked all over Latin America: *¿Dónde están?* Where are they? *¿Dónde están?* That question is written on the walls of churches and courthouses and on cardboard placards carried in hastily organized demonstrations that disperse again just as hastily. It appears on leaflets, and it is sung in the *penas*, the small bars where anyone is free to take up a guitar and sing. When I was in Santiago de Chile two years ago I saw the same question on the wall of the church of Jesus Obrero where forty relatives and friends of the missing lay on cots during a hunger strike, their signs and slogans with them: "Where are they?" "Release them!" "We will find them!"

As of January 1980, conservative estimates set the number of political prisoners in Latin American jails and prison camps at not fewer than seventeen thousand. Many people have been driven into exile. At least thirty thousand have disappeared from 1970 to 1980. The majority of them have probably been murdered. My account is based on conversations I had during my visits to Chile and Argentina. The stories I am passing on are ones I heard from people directly involved. I need not explain why I cannot name the names of abductees, of my sources, or of actual places.

In September 1979, I took part in a hearing in Washington at which witnesses from international organizations appeared before a subcommittee of the House Committee on Foreign Affairs and made statements on the problem of these missing persons and of political abduction. The witnesses belonged to church organizations, the International League for Human Rights, and Amnesty International.

The countries in which abduction has most been used as an instrument of political terror are Argentina, Chile, Uruguay, and El Salvador, which is not to say that it has not been used to a more limited extent in other countries as well. I cannot go into national and historical differences but shall limit myself to sketching the outlines of this phenomenon and to reflecting on it in the light of the personal encounters I had.

Disappearances

"Disappearance" in this new sense means the involuntary disappearance of individuals, in which the government has approved the abduction, conspired in it, or been an accessory to it. Making people disappear is a form of state-imposed terror, an international crime. It is a relatively new phenomenon in the history of state terror. The cases I am discussing here all fall within the decade 1970–1980.

Making someone disappear is different from an ordinary kidnapping because there is no demand for ransom, and no other conditions are set for the victim's release. Disappearance involves capture, abduction, and solitary confinement, and there are reasonable grounds for assuming that the individual who has disappeared was abducted at the orders of a government or of its security or police forces. There is ample evidence of cooperation between the secret services and death squads of different countries. The corpses of people who disappeared in Argentina, for example, have turned up later in Uruguay.

Disappearance is a new criminal fact. We do not even have a word, a descriptive name, for the criminals who make people disappear. We can call them kidnappers, rapists, torturers, or murderers, but those terms do not name this specific crime, this disappearance-making. As a rule the government denies having any part in the crime. Women in Chile were told, for instance, in a snide tone: "Weren't you having marital difficulties? It's not so easy to get a divorce. . . . See if that doesn't give you some clue." It is part of the criminal strategy to admit nothing, to treat disappearances as simple cases of missing persons, and to refer inquiries to another branch of the bureaucracy. The armed forces send someone searching for a relative to the police, but then the police say they do not know anything, and they send the person to a military unit.

Friends and relatives of victims usually refer to the criminals as "they." A friend told me that about five men in civilian clothes came into her apartment at around 2:30 in the morning. She was startled out of her sleep. First they blindfolded her; then they ransacked the whole apartment. Everything happened so quickly that she was not even sure how many secret policemen there were.

"They" came and got him, everyone says. The subject that commits the crime is "they," an anonymous force that can be either the police or the military, wearing a uniform or civilian clothes. These distinctions do not matter any longer.

Is this disappearance-making ordered from above? Is there a plan behind it? Do upper-echelon government officials know what lower-echelon police organizations are doing? It is hard to pin state terrorism down by recourse to the law. In Uruguay, from 1972 to 1980, one out of every fifty citizens was arrested and interrogated, usually without a warrant, and without any incriminating evidence, and often for extended periods of time. The main task for human rights commissions is to unmask the real criminal, who tries to lay the blame on political terrorists.

There is a basic pattern that disappearances follow, with some variation. The kidnappers, usually in civilian clothes, seize their victims at home, on the street, or at work. They are well organized, armed, and trained. The victims are arrested and interrogated. Torture is the rule, not the exception. There is an increasing use of methods that leave no traces behind. Don Jaime Schmirgelt of the Permanent Assembly for Human Rights reports that in his investigations not one person arrested was not tortured. The army, the navy, the air force, and the police have refined their methods. As a NATO general noted, they have combined the techniques that the French OAS used in Algeria and the CIA in Vietnam. In the winter, for example, prisoners are stripped and put under a cold shower for fifteen minutes. Then they are forced to lie down on a cement floor and are beaten. This method leaves no evidence in the form of bruises. Prisoners receive twenty to a hundred blows on their heels. Many die during torture.

Remember! Do not forget our experience in the resistance: if some survive in the underground, that is the same as saying that they succeeded in living. We live there as if we did not know that death is an imminent reality. We cast our lot with life, even if it ultimately means death. And that is the real difference. Happiness: we have known it, we have experienced it. It was present everywhere, in every refuge and hiding place, with the women, men, and children wherever real resistance was offered.

Carmen Castillo, *Santiago de Chile*
(Reinbek: Rowohlt Verlag, 1981)

Regular military or police units do not interfere when someone being abducted calls for help. In some cases, the government gives the security forces unlimited and unsupervised power to arrest, interrogate, imprison, and execute. In other cases, approval of such actions is given tacitly.

As a rule government spokesmen deny any knowledge of these actions. Normal legal channels yield no results, and no one can learn whether those abducted have been killed or imprisoned. Thousands have disappeared in this way as if the earth had swallowed them up. We know nothing of their fate.

Robert J. Cox of the *Buenos Aires Herald*, a newspaper that has been courageously and tenaciously reporting violations of human rights for years now, told me in September 1979 that two persons had just disappeared. At that time the Inter-American Commission for Human Rights (CIDH), which is a part of the Organization of American States, was visiting Argentina for the first time to conduct an on-the-spot investigation of disappearances and murders, prisons and concentration camps, torture centers and police terror. The fact that the commission came to Argentina was in itself a gesture of resistance, and for the first time the Argentine press (not just the English-language *Herald*) ran articles every day on the subject of human rights. But the report that Mr. Cox had received was useless because the relatives of the two victims had made him promise not to publish the victims' names. What that meant in effect was that his report was a nonreport and those persons nonpersons. There is nothing that a newspaper, a human rights commission, or a lawyer can do with information like that. Not only does state terror make people disappear; it also eradicates their names, their personal existence, their legal identity. Anyone who thinks about them must be mad and—the authorities hope—should also disappear. That is exactly what the state wants: the disappearance of nameless individuals whom no one knows.

This kind of nonreport about nonpersons is an everyday occurrence in Argentina. Two days later, the front page of the *Herald* reported the disappearance of a whole family, including its three small daughters—right under the nose, as it were, of the international commission.

The Victims

Who are the victims of these crimes? They come from all classes of society: professors and students, labor leaders and union members. Many of them have never had any political or ideological connections. Others are linked in some way to people who have already disappeared. In December 1977, for example, two French nuns were abducted by the security police merely because they had attended a meeting held by relatives of missing persons. Some disappear because of some personal grudge or mood of the kidnappers. Some are arrested by mistake, tortured, and then released.

I asked a Third World priest who works in a slum, a *villa miserias*, how many of its inhabitants had disappeared. He knew of only one case in his entire district, which had a population of about five thousand. But, he went on, of all the lawyers, teachers, social workers, housewives, students, nurses, and doctors who had come to help his people, not one was around any longer. "Exiled, fled, murdered, disappeared, or so terrified that they don't dare show their faces anymore—I don't know which."

A young teacher working in a *villa miserias* received gifts of school supplies: notebooks, pencils, books. Occasionally she found money in the notebooks, and she used it to buy more supplies for her pupils. She was arrested and sentenced to eight years in prison on the grounds that the terrorist *monteneros* were supporting her school. "Legal" sentencings of this kind occur very rarely; as a rule people simply disappear and are never heard of again.

A woman told me:

> We had friends, decent people, members of the Protestant church. They had three daughters. The two older girls worked in a slum. They were very idealistic, seventeen and eighteen years old. They joined one of these groups. You know what I mean. One night about three o'clock the secret police came for them. The older girl screamed that she couldn't stand to be tortured. She committed suicide by taking a pill. The younger girl was taken away and has not been heard from since. The youngest daughter is still alive.

Whether political activists, dissidents, union members, or just ordinary citizens who still have human feelings and cannot just watch when their neighbors disappear—the government declares all of them enemies of the state. Those who still think for themselves are subversive. It is dangerous to read books by Freud or Marx. Owning a photocopy machine is almost as bad as having stores of dynamite in your house. A general once classified religion, along with *Marxismo-Leninismo-Judaismo*, as a subversive institution. Intellectual oppression is another way of making people disappear: it prepares the way for the actual disappearance of those who have been decreed enemies of the state.

Public Relations against the Truth

The Argentine government is trying to hide the truth from the public both at home and abroad. At the moment it is doing this in three ways that were not initially linked in a coordinated effort: propaganda, new legislation, and increased terror by silence. The gullible—and some members of the German embassy have to be classified as such—think that things have in fact improved somewhat. But in reality the oppression is merely moving into a new phase in which it is using public relations experts, ideologues, and lawyers as front men for the kidnappers and torture specialists.

All the buses and many store windows display an attractive white and blue sticker that says *Los argentinos somos derechos y humanos*—"Argentinians are decent and humane." These stickers started appearing at the time the human rights commission arrived. This was a clever move. The general public was made to think: "Here a bunch of foreigners are coming to tell us we're inhuman and have no respect for the law when in reality we enjoy soccer games just like anyone else and have finally created law and order in our country."

Another aspect of propaganda has to do with "geopolitics." The government is trying to create a new awareness of Argentina's national territory. In the middle of the main street in Buenos Aires imitation border markers have been put up, and on them are signs that say: "Let's march to our borders." There is much talk about the border areas where, of course, soldiers have to be stationed. School classes collect money for the impoverished *campesinos* in the border territories. Plans are developed for settling the border areas, which are to be "argentinized."

The army and the police—and it is becoming more and more difficult for a citizen to tell the difference between them—do

111

not exist just to deal with emergencies. They are permanent representatives of the national community. If there are no enemies in sight, they have to be invented: Chileans, for example, have been proclaimed a threat to Argentina. Geopolitics prepares the way for an ideology of national security to which all else must be subordinated. As a theology student put it, "We are living under a new religion of the state."

All university professors and instructors are obliged to take two hours of geopolitical instruction a week from military personnel. In the schools, any kind of critical thinking is discouraged. Authors who might promote such thinking are struck from reading lists.

A new subject has been introduced for high-school freshmen. It is called *formación moral y cívica* and is designed to imbue students with the state's political doctrine. The constitution is read word for word, often evoking roars of laughter from the students. The religion of the state incorporates snippets of Thomistic doctrine. Officially, this instruction has nothing to do with religion, but "God" is regarded as part of the natural order, and anyone who doubts his existence is on the way to becoming a subversive.

During the Peronist period, instructional materials based on Paulo Freire's ideas were used. As the students, often adults, learned to spell and write the word "milk," they talked about where milk came from, its nutritional value, its distribution, its price, and why it was not available. A young teacher who had used these materials brought them to a friend of mine a little while ago. The teacher said she could not use them anymore, and she felt it was too dangerous to keep these subversive materials in her apartment.

The Missing Declared Dead

Another method of domestic repression is a legislative one. On September 12, 1979, a law went into force that permits a judge to declare a missing person dead after one year. The request can be made by the person's relatives or by the state. This law is retroactive to 1974. If no objections are registered within ninety days, the missing person is considered dead.

I discussed the advantages and disadvantages of this law with a journalist from the *Herald*. He told me about a woman whose husband had been missing for three years. Argentine law prohibits children from leaving the country without the written permission of their father. They cannot even take a vacation across the river into Uruguay. The young woman said she would continue to search for her husband, but the new law gave her and her children more freedom of movement.

The junta took an extremely unclear position on this law. On the one hand, it claimed that human rights organizations had requested a law of this kind. All three groups denied this in the sharpest of terms. But then a government spokesman assured the Inter-American Commission that there were no plans at all for such a law.

It is obvious that the disappearance of several thousand people presents legal problems affecting property and custody of children. In many cases the police had not only looted houses but also signed title over to new owners. The government was notified of these crimes.

It is, however, naive to assume that this new law is designed to help people cope with the difficulties of their situation. The junta's interest in it is political and of a very different intent. This law is meant to put an end to the question of missing persons. The past is to be forgotten, by law. A future without missing persons is to start now after a long dirty war against subversion.

Legally, the key point is the power given to judges. Not only relatives but also the state, in the person of a judge, can request a certification of death. Nothing like this has ever been seen in legal history before, and it does indeed represent a new kind of "final solution." Cardinal Arns of São Paulo called this a law that "makes judges accomplices and henchmen to murderers."

Mute Resistance

Along with legalistic means of this kind, there is an intensification of the terror by silence that is turned against the relatives of the missing. A disappearance is in itself a kind of psychological torture for the victim's relatives. They cannot know for sure if a husband, brother, or daughter is dead, and they have to keep postponing their mourning. They know that their relatives are being tortured, and they hear horrible reports. They hear that some victims have their eyes torn out, but again they cannot know what someone near and dear to them is actually enduring. This mixture of hope and uncertainty is itself an instrument of torture.

A mother in Chile told me about her son, who was twenty-six years old in 1974. He was a respected teacher at the university and a spokesman for the students. When he was fired after the putsch, many sprang to his defense. His mother has reason to believe he is dead. She had been told that she should take food and clothing to him, but she was not admitted to the prison. Eight months after his arrest a friend of his saw him in *Tejas Verde*, a notorious torture center. When the commandant of the center was asked about this young man he said, "If swine like that are here, there is good reason for it." Her brother-in-law, who has good connections with the junta and works with electronic devices, probably torture devices, said to her, "He is dead, along with more than a thousand others. Stop searching for him. There's no point to it." She does not cry; she is proud. "He was hard and he stayed hard. He didn't talk. He didn't name any names. None of his friends was arrested." I asked her what her personal motive was for taking part in a hunger strike. She said she wanted to know the truth. The government should admit that everyone who disappeared after 1974 was murdered.

People with some education or with contacts abroad have a certain advantage, of course, and more reason for hope. The same is not true for rural families, the poor, and the illiterate, when their relatives disappear. Often they say nothing, or they confide in their local priest or they tell military men they happen to know. Human rights organizations, including Amnesty International, never hear about these cases. They assume quite correctly that for every case they hear of, there are three to five that no one ever learns about.

It takes a lot of courage not to be intimidated by terror. Those who wanted to submit petitions to the human rights commission in Buenos Aires gave an impressive demonstration of such courage. Day after day relatives of the missing stood in a line five across and four blocks long—a moving assertion of life in defiance of the government. The secret police photographed them. Passersby insulted them. Police agents tried to provoke them. But they received sympathy, too, some people stopped to ask them why they were standing there.

Terror by Silence

The mother of a friend told me that a North American group had asked her to visit prisoners in the notorious prison in Villa Devoto. She was ready to go, but her daughter persuaded her not to. "You have seven grandchildren in this country."

"I didn't go," she said hesitantly. "Was that wrong of me?" There are endless stories of resistance, of failure to resist, of broken spirits. This explains why the estimates of the missing in Argentina alone vary from fifteen thousand to thirty thousand.

The victims' relatives are all exposed to threats. "Don't do anything if you want to see your husband again." This terror by silence is an important strategy for the state terrorists. Even the victims themselves are subjected to it. Some call their homes and say, "Please don't make any inquiries. I'm pretty well off, given the circumstances. Don't talk to anyone." What should one do in a situation like that? Of those few who do reappear, not many will say in what camps they were held prisoner, and they prefer to keep silent about the tortures they suffered.

A Hungarian pastor knew a colonel in the police. When two of his friends disappeared, he asked the officer to find out what had happened to them. He was successful, and the two prisoners were told that they would have to leave the country. One of them, a Jesuit, woke up in a swampy area near La Plata. He assumes that they rendered him unconscious with an injection and then dropped him out of a helicopter. He called up his Hungarian friend, got a passport, and left the country. He refused to talk about the torture he had undergone.

In its annual report for 1976, the Human Rights Commission of the Organization of American States said: "The status of 'missing person' seems to be a convenient means for circumventing laws created for the express purpose of defending the freedom of the individual, physical inviolability, human dignity, and human life itself."

"They Have to Die So That
Our Country Can Live"

What explanations are offered for such persisting, massive, and cynical violations of human rights? The terrorist governments have developed a number of different tactics. At first everything is simply denied. Put under increasing pressure from the international community, governments will admit that there have been isolated cases in which overzealous officers went too far in the performance of their duties. Regrettably, the governments add, security forces cannot be kept under constant supervision. But despite these admissions, no security officer has ever been punished for excessive actions, such as torturing a prisoner to death.

But there are even more cynical methods for hushing up disappearances. Since May 1979, some relatives of missing persons in Chile have been receiving letters containing death threats. A woman whose husband disappeared in August 1976 received this note in the mail: "It is pointless for you to try to find out where your husband is. We killed him in April 1977 and threw his body, with many others, into the sea. We killed him because he was a communist and a traitor to his country. You too are as good as dead."

According to Comando Carevic, these death letters were signed "An eye for an eye." Carevic was an army lieutenant who was killed by a bomb explosion in 1979. Five months before General Videla assumed the presidency he announced: "There will be as many deaths in Argentina as are necessary to restore law and order."

The "dirty war" against subversion, against the extreme left, against terrorists, is always cited as the official legitimation of government terror. In an Argentine newspaper I saw an advertisement sympathetic to the government and directed against terror from the left. Three hundred relatives of victims of leftist terrorists had signed the ad. The ad pointed out that before the military had seized power no one on the street could feel safe from bombs and explosions. According to the highest estimates, terrorist activities on the part of this group were responsible for the deaths of about a thousand persons. Most of the victims were prominent figures: business leaders, police chiefs, military men, politicians.

The present government says that this wave of terror forced it, to its regret, to resort to drastic measures too. But now, the ad also stressed, peace and order have been restored.

But this explanation is inadequate and self-contradictory. According to this logic of reprisal, the state's terror should have ceased long ago. If it is true that terror by silence has increased recently because neither propaganda nor laws alone have created enough repression, then we have to find other reasons for state terror and the continuation of systematic torture. What really underlies this terror is economic necessity, not just the excesses of a few crazed sadists. Torture and abduction can be traced back to economic causes.

Since the coup, wages in Argentina have dropped by at least one half. Both the unions and the national interest group of industrialists were disbanded. As isolated, local groups, the unions have practically no power at all. According to the minister of commerce, Martin de Hoz, the nation's industry is not working efficiently enough. He is planning increased economic concentration and monopolization of industry. Credit and investment policy will favor multinational concerns. Financially, dependence on the World Bank and the International Monetary Fund (IMF), whose boards are dominated by the United States, will be increased. Argentinians just do not work hard enough, de Hoz says. Therefore, they have to be exposed to international competition and learn to measure up in it.

This economic policy is visibly manifest in everyday life. In retail stores everywhere, goods are advertised with the only remaining label of quality there is: imported. All import duties have been removed in an effort to make Argentine industry competitive. In the opinion of Argentina's economic leaders, who all cite Milton Friedman of Chicago as their authority, the domestic market is insufficient. The liberalization of imports will lead, for all practical purposes, to the destruction of Argentina's industrial sector. A union leader says of this policy that it will destroy the work of Argentina's middle class for the last four generations. When small firms go bankrupt, the multinational concerns jump in and buy them up.

It is essential to all these maneuverings that the organized working class be destroyed. Argentine workers experienced better times under Perón. They reject military dictatorship and large rural landholdings, and for twenty-three years they have resorted to strikes, sabotage, and riots to combat the forces that want to collaborate with foreign capital. In recent years there have been wildcat strikes, sit-down strikes, and work slowdowns time and again. In early June, a strike by railroad workers paralyzed the entire transit system around Buenos Aires.

There is resistance; therefore, there must be terror. The government had to resort to terror to halve the wages of a labor force that has been organized for generations.

According to the plans of the minister of commerce, Argentina should play the role envisioned for it in the international division of labor worked out by the Trilateral Commission. This role is to develop means of agricultural production advanced enough to give Argentina entry into international agribusiness.

The present wave of repression has to be seen in the context of this economic plan that will eradicate local industry and set the country back fifty years. The prohibition on thought and the persecution of psychiatrists and lawyers who resist is not the only sign of scorn for human rights. An organized working class cannot be tolerated, and the middle-echelon leadership of the workers' movement has been liquidated. Unlike Chile, Argentina has spared a few top figures in the unions and the leftist parties, while stamping out the ranks below them all the more radically.

"They have to die so that our country can live." That is the murderers' motto. Their goal is to annihilate the activists so that all memory of resistance and the historical experience of freedom movements will be removed.

The Torturers

Those who reflect on these thousands of disappearances and on systematic torture will find themselves driven to the outer limits of intellectual and emotional comprehension. How can human beings do such things?

A friend of mine who was being interrogated in Argentina screamed at her torturers: "Do you call yourselves Christians?" The men had their fun with the young woman who stood before them blindfolded. One of them unbuttoned his shirt, took her hand, and laid it on his chest. "There, feel that," he yelled at her. It was a swastika he was wearing around his neck. Another man said, "We're not as bad as all that," and he had her touch a cross that he wore. The two symbols had become interchangeable.

There is a horrifying document that reveals something of the psychology of those who consider national security the most important political concept. It is a letter written by the Brazilian police commissioner in São Paulo, Sergio Fleury, in November 1977. A group of French Christians working for the abolition of torture had written to twenty-one known torturers. Their letter said, among other things: "You are learning outright sadism. . . . You are tools in the hands of those who want to maintain a grossly unjust social order at any price. . . . You are destroying yourselves; you are destroying the victims you torture; and you are destroying the country you want to defend. . . . You may someday find these dreadful practices turned against your own person. . . . Stop today!"

In his long response, the torture specialist does not discuss the question of torture at all. In a kind of animal fable about an eagle that hatches only chicken eggs, he contrasts his political ideology with that of the French letter writers who still think in Christian, socialistic, and democratic terms.

"The eagle continues to hope that one day, among the flocks of shortsighted and cackling chickens, a young eagle will appear that can be its companion. The eagle has not given up hope yet, and it continues to raise chicks, protecting and defending them with its mighty wings (for that is the eagle's mission in life). Anyone who does not want to become an eagle and fears the eagle will be one of the herd and be devoured with the herd."

This imagery from the animal world openly glorifies power and strength. These are the only values it is worth living for. Fleury writes: "Don't be 'upset,' my 'little gentleman,' 'little chief of the democrats and proletarians of the whole world.' Just answer me this question: Why have you never been able to come to power? Or, on those few occasions when you have won power, why have you always yielded it again to someone else?"

The power that needs torture to crush subversion in any form is justified in and of itself. I need not elaborate here on the blindness that prevented this power-mad fascist from seeing that he was nothing but a small functionary within a much larger concentration of power than he realized. For him, the world is a battle between eagles and chicks, and he has decided which side he wants to be on.

The letter of the young Christians ends with the sentence: "We are fully aware—and this is the thought we want to leave you with—that we belong to the same human race as you." The torturer adds as a postscript: "I do not think—I have to admit—that we are members of the same human race."

When I think about the flouting of human rights in Latin America, I am tempted to feel that the torturer is right. It seems impossible to me to recognize a torturer as a fellow human being. But then I have to listen again to the voices of those who continue to resist and do not give up. They do not let themselves be overwhelmed by fear or hatred. A leaflet from Chile bears the title: "Don't Let Them Steal Your Soul Away" (see below, p. 127).

Questions for Us

The simplest questions cannot be asked too often. What does all this have to do with us? Is it true that human rights are indivisible? In what sense is a failure to render aid a violation of human rights? Is the maximizing of profits a violation of human rights if others have to do the dirty work? The mother of a girl who disappeared in Argentina received a shoebox in the mail. In it were her daughter's hands.

The goal of Amnesty International is to ostracize torture so much in the international community that it will become "as unthinkable as slavery." The problem is, though, that we are dealing with a new form of slavery here, one that needs torture to exist. Slavery, total dependence, is the goal of the silent war we are engaged in now, the war of the rich against the poor. Torture is nothing more than a method of breaking down resistance against economic subjugation.

In 1972, a barrel of oil cost the equivalent of twenty-six kilos of bananas in the Third World. Today, that same barrel costs 200 kilos of bananas. What will rural workers in the year 2000 be getting for their products? Participation in the world market, forced on the poor countries by the industrialized ones, and the destruction of domestic markets are facts of life everywhere in the

In the train

"CAPITAL" TELLS YOU EVERY MONTH
HOW TO GET THE MOST OUT OF YOUR
MONEY AND YOUR JOB

The gray-green pastures in schleswig
a train like this doesn't go very fast
behind the words of the ad
I can see the huge sun above the edge of the meadow
behind MONEY and JOB a cluster of trees
there must be a farm over there

The brownish red dried-up trees
draw me closer but
"CAPITAL" tells me every day
how I can GET THE MOST
out of the gently grazing clouds
there must once have been a farm over there

When oedipus was at the point where I am
the heavens desolated
the earth prostituted
he blinded himself
to learn how to see

Third World. This is the silent war of the rich against the poor. In many fertile areas in Latin America where rice, corn, and beans used to be raised there are plantations belonging to multinational corporations. The crops raised there are strawberries and orchids, both intended for export. The local population goes hungry, children become feeble-minded from lack of protein, the elderly die, and young adults leave the country. For whom are these strawberries and orchids raised? Who profits from them? The very people who do not trouble themselves about all this.

The situation in the Federal Republic of Germany often strikes me as analogous to that of the Americans in the early years of the Vietnam war when the Americans had their allies—Koreans, for example—torture prisoners and civilians while they stood by with tape recorders to get the strategically important information they wanted. Are our economic leaders doing anything different when their business partners in Chile and Argentina instigate the disappearance of those who have been declared subversives and enemies of the state?

In our country the conspiracy of silence is taken for granted. The absence of public discussion on international issues of human rights is regarded as normal. An editor at a West German broadcasting company learned recently that Cardinal Arns of São Paulo, Brazil, regularly hands on to the BBC the names of missing persons that he receives from national human rights groups in Latin America. The BBC then announces these names on the air. The editor wondered whether this might not be possible for German radio stations too, this human and political minimum of at least mentioning on the radio the names of those who are probably being tortured or murdered at that very moment. When asked if this could be done, none of the editors at that radio station felt they were competent to make that decision. The question was politically too sensitive. The director of the station would not even discuss the matter.

The leaflet from the Chilean underground that I mentioned before, the one addressed "to those who are on the verge of resignation and whose commitment is flagging," says in part:

> This represents the greatest danger for us at the moment, but it is also a great danger for our children and the coming

generations: this loss of moral sensitivity, this willed or at least accepted confusion between good and evil. There are things that we must cry out against in the depths of our souls even if we cannot mention them aloud on the street. Otherwise we will forget about them. We are writing these lines so that you will not forget these things but will instead wake up and blaze like a torch.

But who in the First World, where these things originate, hears such words? It strikes me as cynical to dismiss them as "mere moral rhetoric." Those who talk like that destroy themselves, let their "souls be stolen away." We know that in the Union of South Africa young whites in the suburbs tend to know nothing or very little about the living conditions of blacks their own age. Reports about the lack of electricity and running water in most of the shacks in Soweto are considered fabrications. In this way, intellectual apartheid, an apartheid of information, is maintained. And the West German situation, manipulated as it is by media policy, is identical. The vast majority of our population lives in apartheid, enjoys a culture of apartheid. For us apartheid knowledge, apartheid feelings, and apartheid ideology are normal. It is hard to explain why some people choose not to eat Outspan oranges (from South Africa). Apartheid becomes a state of mind.

In recent months economic relations between the Federal Republic of Germany and Chile have experienced a new boom. Our country is the world's major buyer of Chilean goods; our banks are supporting the Pinochet regime with loans in the millions; large concerns such as Krupp are looking for new investment possibilities in Chile; and our government has sent an expert in economics and finance to Santiago as our new ambassador.

Pinochet is receiving support of a special order from the Hanns Seidel Foundation of the CSU, which—in the wake of Franz-Josef Strauss's goodwill visit to Chile—has become a consultant to the fascists in the training of union members loyal to the regime and in framing a new Chilean constitution.

Chilean Foreign Minister Cubillos claimed during his visit to the Federal Republic in September 1979 that there were no infringements of human rights in Chile, and we hear numerous reports of "improvements" in the Chilean situation. Cubillos's claim and these reports are not true. The political and social repression in Chile remains basically unchanged today, more than nine years after the bloody putsch of September 11, 1973.

Now as before, there are arbitrary arrests, political prisoners, torture, and murder. These are facts documented by the Vicaria de la Solidaridad. Now as before, all political parties and activities are forbidden. Laws are enacted to further weaken the labor movement. After more than nine years, the fate of missing political prisoners remains unknown. Worse still, police officers who were proved in court to have murdered a group of missing persons were acquitted under the so-called amnesty law.

Never before has there been such high unemployment in Chile. Official government figures set it at 13 percent. In reality, it is about 25 percent. Public expenditures for health care and education are being cut continually. Between September 1978 and September 1979 the cost of living rose 48 percent. Increases in the cost of staples have been particularly high. The price of potatoes has increased 87.5 percent; of beans, 223 percent. When the price controls on bread were lifted in the fall of 1977, the price rose 176 percent.

The idea that we should cut off economic cooperation to protest violations of human rights seems to be beyond the comprehension of West German business leaders. In September 1979, three SPD representatives from the *Bundestag* went to Argentina and Uruguay on a fact-finding mission. The statement they made to the press on their return left much to be desired: ''Both countries have suffered heavily from terrorism [and here terrorism from the left is meant]. Success has been achieved in the necessary struggle against violent crime of terrorist nature. But the price for the restoration of internal security has been high. Even if the difficult domestic political circumstances are taken into account, lapses and excesses have occurred that violate basic constitutional principles.'' This kind of language (lapses, excesses) reflects that of the generals. Behind it lies the theory of a dirty war that, unfortunately, makes dirty methods of retaliation necessary. The *Bundestag* representatives concluded that ''the return of both states to a democratic order seems possible.''

When I spoke, at about that same time, with the mother of Klaus Zieschank, who has been missing since 1976, I hardly had the impression that she had been encouraged by the interview she had just had with Count Lambsdorff. There is not the faintest indication that the Federal Republic will impose economic sanctions, even if German citizens are among the missing. Next to no pressure is being brought to bear either through diplomatic, journalistic, or economic channels.

Systematized World Injustice

West Germany has delivered an atomic power plant to Argentina, and it will soon deliver two to Brazil. The unproblematic relationships that the Federal Republic maintains with most of the terrorist states in the economic sector have their repercussions not only on our media policies but also, I feel, on the individual psyche in our country. Apartheid as an economic, political, and cultural strategy cannot be practiced in such a way that it leaves the rich and privileged classes on this side of the barrier unharmed. Just as a master who needs a slave cannot be free, so the citizens of a country that profits from the apartheid imposed on others cannot be free. Outspan oranges do in fact taste of blood. The involvement in profits that are maintained by exploitation and torture, the failure to render aid, the quashing of certain information, all these things strike back with the logic of repression, for whatever is repressed will return and take vengeance.

"There is no such thing as foreign suffering," the Soviet writer Konstantin Simonov said during the Vietnam war. At first, I interpreted this sentence only in the context of the tradition of sympathy. But it can also be understood in a Freudian sense: the suffering of others that I refuse to recognize and that I make alien to myself will become my own unconscious suffering. The material poverty in the Third World takes its toll psychologically in the First World. The disappearance of others that we watch happen and that we profit from indirectly will make us disappear too.

I am afraid of the year 2000. A world system of injustice like this affects the psyche of every one of us. The Federal Republic already has the highest rate of child suicide in the world, five hundred per year. About eighty thousand of our young people are drug addicts. Forty percent of our students are in psychotherapy or seeking psychotherapeutic care. The psychic misery that surrounds us goes hand in glove with our economic, political, and intellectual situation. We export weapons and atomic technology, but is it only profit that we derive from it? Does not the death that we export strike back at us?

Foreign observers are often struck by the coldness of human relationships in the Federal Republic. The workers who know how meaningless their work is, the men and women who suffer from the emptiness and interchangeability of their relationships, the children and young people who are aggressive and destructive toward others and themselves—they all reveal domestic repercussions of our foreign policy, the psychic consequences of an economic scheme.

Economics, politics, and culture make up a unity. Psychotherapeutic methods that neglect that unity and focus only on the inner life produce nothing but psychological dependency. Psychology today is the opium of the middle class, an opium that denies this unity. We can learn more from the resistance of oppressed peoples who, with their simple, old-fashioned ("moral") language, speak for us too and help us organize resistance.

"Chile, awaken! Don't let them steal your soul away! Your freedom-loving spirit sang other songs before. Will it sing songs of freedom and justice again someday? Pay attention to how your children are being educated, what they are being taught. Otherwise, things will get so far out of hand—while you sleep—that someone will tell them it is good to kill your brother, that it is good to believe what the official press says, that truth is a lie, that lies are truth" (Chilean leaflet).

Don't Let Them Steal Your Soul Away

*An Appeal from the Chilean Underground to
Those Who Are on the Verge of Resignation
and Whose Commitment Is Flagging*

Document

*The following text, which has been circulating in the Chilean
underground since April 1980, made its way to Germany by way of
trustworthy go-betweens. It was written by a so-called Christian
reflection group in Valparaiso. Made up of lay persons and
Catholic priests who have sided with the resistance against military
dictatorships in Latin America, this group comes together in
spontaneous, unpublicized meetings.*

Soon we will all be ready to throw in the towel. What used to
electrify us or outrage us not long ago now leaves us unmoved and
passive.

This represents the greatest danger for us now, but it is also a
great danger for our children and the coming generations: this loss
of moral sensitivity, this willed or at least accepted confusion
between good and evil. There are things that we must cry out
against in the depths of our souls even if we cannot mention them
aloud on the street. Otherwise we shall forget about them. We are
writing these lines so that you will not forget these things but will
instead awaken and blaze like a torch.

They do not come as a harbinger of war but of peace, not of
weakness but of strength.

We call it a loss of moral sensitivity that we accept as normal that
hundreds of thousands of Chileans have to live in exile simply
because they do not think the way the men in power do or because

their homeland does not give them enough to eat. These men and women and these children who in the meantime have learned other languages in the countries that have taken them in still belong to us; they are our flesh and blood. With what right have we abandoned them? Who issued the order to divide Chile and spread it over the entire world?

We demand for all Chileans the minimal right to be able to live in their own country.

Furthermore, that hundreds of Chileans have disappeared without a trace represents an incredible breach of morality. We are told, of course, that everything has been clarified, but in reality nothing has been clarified. Mothers and wives are still standing here with eyes dried up from weeping and feet tired from all their searching, but despite this they are unbroken in their will to insist that justice be done.

But what about us? How can it be that we calmly go about our business and simply forget so many atrocities?

Chile, awaken! But not to seek vengeance or to murder. Awaken, so that you will be found ready to demand what belongs to you. Awaken, so that your soul, dignity, and joy cannot be stolen from you. Anyone who has the effrontery to say that the economy is beginning to improve while huge numbers of people are suffering from dreadful poverty is either immoral or joking. What we are experiencing now is hardly helping our economy to recover.

It is immoral to silence a people and bar the way to its future. It is an insult to tell people they are immature or intellectually limited and others will have to make the necessary decisions for them. Have we not accustomed ourselves to all these things? What are we telling our children? That freedom is the snow of last winter? We lost it, and they will never regain it? Or are we telling them they will have to reconquer it themselves? But with what right do we tell them this?

We have accustomed ourselves to having a humiliated and servile working class. Workers cannot assemble freely, cannot elect their leaders, cannot defend themselves with the weapon proper to them—the strike. They cannot organize nationally. But all these things are permitted to the entrepreneurs. Are they supposedly good and the others bad? The entrepreneurs are innocent, and the workers are criminals?

Awaken, Chile! Do not let them steal your soul away. Your freedom-loving spirit sang other songs before. Will it sing songs of freedom and justice again someday? Pay attention to how your children are being educated, what they are being taught. Otherwise, things will get so far out of hand—while you sleep—that someone will tell them it is good to kill your brother, that it is good to believe what the official press says, that truth is a lie, that lies are truth.

And what are we to make of this climate of secrecy? What is the meaning of this secret police that sullies itself with blood in Santiago at night? Why these unexplained deaths in foreign countries? Chileans, you are not being told the truth. You will never be told the truth, for the father of lies rules in our country. Let them go on telling lies, but you must not let them infect your soul.

Not long ago you were summoned to a referendum. On the morning of that day they fetched the poor out of their houses at daybreak. They were threatened with losing everything they had if they did not vote. The rich turned up in our towns and saw to it that the poor did what they were supposed to do. They made the ballots out of transparent paper and tried to tell the people that the ballot was secret. That evening they celebrated their triumph and had their fun.

Chile, awaken! Distorting the meaning of "amnesty" and calling for "Christian reconciliation," they are about to let the torturings, kidnappings, and murders committed by the security forces—which is to say, their own crimes—go unpunished. Chile, keep your eyes open for all their complicity and hypocrisy! If you stop thinking, they will soon be laughing at you again. If you do not do what history demands of you, if you do not join with others to take your future into your own hands, they will soon be laughing at you again.

Chile, awaken! When you are awake, you will be able to look at your countryside and your cities, at your men and women. You will set out on your path and do your part to build a new nation, a nation of brothers and sisters. Only then will your flag not be flecked with blood when it bears the color of your country in the spring. Chile, awaken and stand tall!

Chicken feed

Dog food josé writes me from the *villa miserias*
is too expensive for many peruvians
they're buying chicken feed to thicken their soup

How many more times must we hear these stories
how often repeat news reports like these
in which the media people say there is nothing newsworthy

Is seven times enough one of the disciples asked jesus
please spread the news as long as things remain unchanged
seven times seventy times over we must tell this story

There will come a time when we won't hear it any longer
there will be a land where it will no longer be true
chicken feed will once again be a slang expression

For small change and things not worth the bother
then we'll send the editors april fool's telegrams
spread the news as long as you remain unchanged

A Story from Chile

A Presbyterian minister from the south of Chile distributed food
that he had received from friends in North America. He was
arrested and put in the Los Alamos prison in Santiago. A hundred
and fifty men were held prisoner there in a building not much
bigger than a two-car garage. He took on the role of prison
chaplain, holding Bible study groups and worship services every
day for his fellow prisoners, most of whom were socialists. He
never had a congregation like that one, he said. When he was
released, his fellow prisoners wrote their names on his back with
burnt-out matches. It was November and warm. He was released
without being stripped and searched, and he went to the Peace
Committee. Most of the names, names of people who had been
given up for lost, could still be read.

The names appear again, written with matches on the back of a
prisoner. The time of silence is over, Don Jaime Schmirgelt told us.
For the first time the political parties in Argentina—the Peronist
and the radical party—have taken up the cause of human rights.
Those are signs of hope that cannot be eradicated by the threat of
torture, by the terror of silence, or by the milder terror of our
forgetfulness.

I travel around to speak about god

I travel around to speak about god
and begin as a matter of course
with the ogre
and ask my listeners
not to serve him any longer
not to go on sacrificing
their labor and their children to him
their short lives

Softly I speak the language of remembrance
of a life without fear of being eaten alive
and touch once more with my hands
the great old words
I speak of the women in the soviet union as sisters
and when the hungry are fed I say peace
and I don't apologize
for having nothing to say
about the ogres in other lands

Because after all I was invited
to speak about god

To Love Means Not to Hide

I was in Santiago de Chile from June 1 to 5, 1978, to inform myself firsthand about the hunger strike that relatives of about twenty-five hundred missing persons had organized there. About two hundred people were taking part in this strike: relatives of missing persons, political prisoners in the Penitenciaría prison, union members, priests, and nuns. The strike began on May 22, and most of the strikers had gone without food for over two weeks.

I had my doubts and reservations about accepting the invitation, extended by the organization Chile Democrático in Rome, to go to Chile as a member of an international delegation. What good can come of this? I asked myself. The women on whose behalf I will visit Chile are sleeping on mattresses on the stone floors of churches. I will stay in a hotel. They wear, pinned to their clothes, photos of their missing husbands, sons, and friends. I will return to my family. They put their physical existence on the line in this struggle. I fight only with my typewriter and my voice. They do what they are doing at the risk of their lives. They are ready to accept the direst consequences. It is possible that those who are speaking out for the missing now will themselves be kidnapped later. The worst that can happen to me is that I will be forced to leave the country and have to go through some unpleasantness with the authorities. In short: they are starving while I eat.

I still have not found any satisfactory answers to these questions. What do we really mean when we use that grand word "solidarity"? How do we leave the noun behind and find the right verb? A prisoner gave me a silver medallion with the inscription on it, "*como si posible aprisionar el aire*—as if it were possible to imprison the air," a line from Neruda, I think. And I read in that line, as the minimum of solidarity we are obliged to muster, the categorical imperative never, under any circumstances, to make our peace with what has happened and is happening, never to be bribed into forgetfulness.

We were in three of the seven churches in which hunger strikes were being held, and we talked to many of the people who were refusing to eat. We asked the same question over and over again: Why are you here? What is your motivation? What do you want? A young girl with broad Indian features said:

> My father was kidnapped in 1976 on his way to work. We waited for him that evening, but he didn't come back. Then a neighbor told us that he had been picked up. We haven't heard anything since then. None of our letters or petitions has done any good. My mother is working to support the family—five children. So I decided to go on this hunger strike for my father.

She is twenty-two years old. On her twelfth day in the strike she complains of a headache.

"Will you give up?" I ask her.

"Not until we know what happened to him. They have to tell us."

The strikers drink three liters of warm water a day to prevent colds; they take salt and vitamins. All of them are under medical supervision. Most of them are women, and they define themselves in terms of their relationships: I am the mother of . . . the girl friend of . . . the daughter of. . . .

In the women's movement we have been trying for a long time to rid ourselves of this kind of self-definition, but here it has a very different meaning. "To love means not to hide," we hear that evening in a *pena*, a gathering in a small bar where songs are sung to the guitar. Anyone in the crowd can pick up the guitar and sing. They drink wine and listen. The *pena* has always been a vehicle for political critique. Love songs are sung here and songs of the *campesinos*, the rural laborers. Today these songs take the form of cultural resistance, like the song about a missing person, a young man who went out one day and never came back, songs of the freedom fighters from all over Latin America.

The first *pena* we wanted to go to still had its ad in the newspaper, but it had just been shut down by the government. We went to another *pena* and heard a song about love, but not just about "you and me" in love:

134

Love—with your face to the sun, no hiding
Love—giving your life every minute
Love—going unmasked, showing your face
Love—risking your life for your people
I cannot live without loving.

But to come back to the church where the strikers lie next to each other in two long rows on the floor. Some medical students are visiting. They have with them a resolution of solidarity that can get every one of them who has signed thrown out of the university. There are twelve hundred names. They play guitars and sing. Most of the women are knitting. Some leaf through magazines.

A woman suddenly unpins the photograph of her son from her dress and gives it to me. His ID number, 551054 2 STGO, is on the photograph. A young man who was twenty-six years old in 1974. He taught at the Poid Institute and was a highly respected teacher.

I ask an old Jesuit priest why he is striking. He says he has seen too many dead bodies in the river. He sees two possible ways for the cardinal to mediate between the strike committee and the present government. If the government admits to the murder of the twenty-five hundred missing persons, it will not be able to stay in power. But it is also possible that it will appoint an investigating committee that will find out where the missing are, who was killed and under what circumstances, and what has happened to those whose fate is uncertain. This old priest—one of seven clergymen and six nuns who are not relatives of missing persons—will soon celebrate his seventy-first birthday.

Morale here in the church of Jesus Obrero is particularly good. The strikers have made a birthday cake out of toilet paper, lit a candle, and sung "Happy Birthday" for one of the nuns. Over a hundred letters and telegrams arrive every day, many of them from the Federal Republic of Germany. The government declares it will not negotiate as long as the strikers continue to fast and—two days later—that the strike leaders will be held responsible for all the consequences of the strike.

A theological colleague discusses with me the significance of this broad popular movement. "Nowhere but in Chile could this happen. It is essential for the growth of our country. Half of our population feel paralyzed by guilt because of their silence, their forgetfulness, their fear," he says. "Now we are experiencing an awakening. There is a feeling of intense happiness here. Theology makes sense only here, in the midst of the popular movement. The hunger strike is a *locus theologicus*. We understand each other.''

The fasting is taking its toll physically, but the mood, the feeling, is high. The British consul was here yesterday, and he was weeping when he left. Night vigils, prayers, readings of pastoral letters take place throughout the night. A 16-year-old girl, the daughter of a missing person, and her friends are organizing a day of fasting and prayer, her mother tells me. A few days ago a Mass was celebrated in which an analogy to the fate of Aldo Moro was drawn: ''There are more than two thousand Aldo Moros here,'' the celebrant pointed out, but they are not prominent figures. It would be very helpful if the pope would intercede on their behalf.

Religious expression and political struggle merge here. This is the very thing that irritates the junta at the same time that it makes the tactically rather cautious cardinal uneasy. He tried to prevent the strike from spreading and seems out of touch with the popular base of the movement, unlike Suffragan Bishop Enrique Alvear, who visits the strikers twice a day.

The political significance of this hunger strike on the part of relatives of the missing has to be seen in a double context: the context of the junta's own increasing weakness, insecurity, and internal disunity, and the context of the people's resistance, which is taking more open and conscious forms now than it did a year earlier.

We spoke with a union leader who, together with some writers and musicians, was visiting the strikers in Don Bosco. Speaking for a hundred thousand copper workers, he said that the hunger strike represented what the majority of the people wanted. At the moment, the government is suppressing the majority by ''legal'' measures, such as the repeal of civil rights and labor laws, and by illegal methods such as exile and arrest.

An important role for the unions in the broader movement, of which the hunger strike is one manifestation, is keeping communications open. Because of their efforts, the strike is spreading beyond Santiago, and strikes for the missing are being held in Concepción and Valparaiso too. The unions have sent their members into other areas of the country to spread the news of the strike where ''foreign'' radio stations, as everyone calls them—Radio Moscow, Havana, or East Berlin—cannot be received. The hunger strike no longer has the character of an isolated and bourgeois means of struggle. "It will go on," as the union leader said, "until a solution is found, and that solution will have to be a political one if thinking workers are to be satisfied."

The organization of resistance after the putsch has gone through different phases. By 1976 all the democratic organizations of the working class that were destroyed by the putsch had managed to reorganize. These unions, underground parties, and solidarity movements have been functioning effectively again since that time. Fear is subsiding; there has been a change in the climate. Now the junta cannot afford, for example, to just make the hunger strikers disappear. I do not mean to say that the period of state terrorism is over, but the strike does represent a broad, growing, and increasingly visible resistance movement. The junta cannot just eradicate the movement, and because of its relatively weak position it is hesitant to make decisions. It is clear that the cases of missing persons cannot be cleared up as long as the military government is in power.

Visit to La Penitencería

The preliminary talk necessary for a visit in La Penitencería ends in an outburst of giggles and whispers among four women. It turns out that no woman will be allowed inside without a skirt and slip. Although we, as foreigners, encountered no difficulties in getting into this prison where thirty-one political prisoners are being detained, still, as women, we have to put on the proper disguise: jeans off, bras on. Our Chilean friends, who want to visit their husbands, are as amused as we are.

Two female guards search us briefly, and after we have turned in our passports we are let inside and walk into a long, narrow, cellarlike area with about a hundred people in it. Thirty-one of them are prisoners who are not officially classified as political prisoners. Accused of theft and assault, they are militant members of leftist parties, and most of them have been in prison since 1976 or 1977. All thirty-one are participating in the hunger strike.

Trying to keep our questioning brief because we realize that they want to spend the two-hour visiting period with their wives, we ask some of them why they are on the hunger strike. All of them were arrested and abducted either at work, on their way home, or when their houses were searched. All of them had been at torture centers before they were brought to La Penitencería where the sanitation is catastrophically bad but where torture is not practiced. When they were arrested, interrogated, and subjected to torture that lasted for days, sometimes even for weeks, they met many others like themselves who are now on the lists of the missing. They know of many who were murdered, and they know that they could just as well be among the missing themselves. The connections with other concentration camps, prisons, and torture centers are good, the degree of organization high.

These prisoners were participating in the hunger strike for personal and political reasons, and in view of their poor state of health, this participation was proof of their moral strength and superiority. In that damp, cellarlike room, inadequately heated with four small stoves, those fasting prisoners and their visitors created an atmosphere that defies description. I have never seen so much open tenderness exchanged in any group before. Gestures of affection—mute, mournful, and heartening—passed between lovers, between man and wife, between mother and son. A father, like most of the strikers, probably too weak to stand sat on a bench. His daughter of about ten stood between his knees. He stroked her hair, touched her face. A very old man, a visitor, went from one prisoner to another, nodded to them or spoke a few words. He was treated with the greatest respect by all of them. Before the strike, these prisoners had been doing craftwork, making baskets, jewelry, and other such items.

The government recently denied once more, as it consistently has, the existence of political prisoners and the fact that these same prisoners are on a hunger strike. The Vicaria de la Solidaridad responded with a denial of the government claim and has published a report of the prisoners' state of health. Their medical care has been wretched since February 1978 when a new director was appointed to the International Red Cross office in Santiago. According to several prisoners, this new director deals exclusively with the mayor and the top prison officials. The prisoners called the Red Cross's performance "criminal." Some strikers who staged their hunger strike in the office of the Red Cross were kept in total isolation and could not have any visitors or receive mail.

A letter

The small twin-engine plane with sixteen seats
is flying over ice-covered lakes and black forests
now we are veering toward the first rays of the sun
I'd like to write a letter to simone weil
my sister
I'd like to share the early morning moon with you
and roll out the sun for you
it is not true
that one has to starve to death
in the love for god called resistance
eat I say goddamnit

They were, however, visited three times a day by a doctor, who impressed on them how weak and frail they were.

They had no mattresses. Two *carabineros* guarded them constantly, and the Red Cross director regarded them as a personal nuisance. After all, his office is no hospital. Members of this group have in the meantime broken off their strike or are now in the hospital.

As the prisoners see it, the amnesty the junta announced in April 1978 had three objectives: (1) to improve the junta's image abroad; (2) to guarantee the torturers belonging to the DINA (*Dirección de Inteligencia Nacional*, National Intelligence Administration— secret police) freedom from punishment; and (3) to make it possible for the junta to release prisoners. In the prison of Santiago, three were released but were then picked up again immediately by the DINA and taken to torture centers.

Another of the junta's tricks is to close down certain concentration camps and announce that the camps are no longer needed. In reality, however, the camps are simply moved to new, secret locations.

Public Resistance

We were eyewitnesses to a demonstration of the new political consciousness. On June 3 at about 12:30 P.M. we saw a silent protest march of about 120 people move through the downtown area toward the supreme court building and place their cardboard signs and posters at the entrance. "Paz Amor Justicia" the signs read. "We will find them." "Where are the missing?" We jumped out of our car and joined the group, which was regarded by passersby with a mixture of fear and deep respect. In front of the court building, the group dispersed. A cluster of about twenty people, mostly young, formed around us. The police moved in on us.

A young woman began to sing Beethoven's "Hymn to Joy." We sang two verses, she in Spanish, we in German, and it became clear to me once again that the best elements of the great middle-class tradition of liberation live on today in the Third World's struggle against the feudalism represented by the First World. "All will be brothers." Why, I asked myself, do I have to fly to Chile to sing *Freude schöner Götterfunken* on the street? Why has the best of our tradition never been seized upon, never been taken up by everyone?

Matilda Neruda, Pablo's widow, wrote in a letter of solidarity:

Dear Friends,

Today is your eighth day on the path you have chosen to follow. This path may prove fatal for you, but you have preferred to take it rather than to live in constant fear for those you love. I know almost all of you. You have told me your tragedies, and together with you and with a mother who lost her pregnant daughter, I have asked myself a thousand times over: Where is my grandson or granddaughter who must have been born by now? Where is the husband of my friend here who longs for him day after day? Where are the children, the brothers, the husbands, the wives, the fiancés of the despairing? Where are they?

Pablo Neruda's grave is not easy to find in the most remote corner of the graveyard. Neither is Victor Jara's. But it is visited often nonetheless. There are almost always flowers on it. The outrage over the junta's barbarity toward Chile's greatest poet is universal even in upper-middle class circles, and it expresses itself in unrestrained weeping and loud cursing.

We were told about another example of growing public resistance. On March 8, 1978, several thousand spectators were present at a program celebrating International Women's Day in the Teatro Caupolican. The cry of "Viva Pablo Neruda!" raised by one person evoked the response, "Pablo Neruda, *¡presente!*" from the whole crowd. Someone else called out, "Viva Victor Jara!" Again the response: "Victor Jara, *¡presente!*" Then someone called out "Viva Salvador Allende!" There was a second of silence; then the crowd stood up and shouted, "Salvador Allende, *¡presente!*"

On May 1, 1978, a demonstration organized jointly by the unions, the Christian Democrats, and the Unidad Popular drew a crowd estimated at between six thousand and eight thousand. About six hundred demonstrators were arrested but soon released.

The days of the junta, or at least of Pinochet, may well be numbered. For now, that remains a matter of speculation. But what I find new and important is that the general population is refusing to accept that the missing are, as a camp commander put it, "just plain gone and that's that." Unlike the Germans under Nazism, the Chileans have not made peace with the fact that people disappear and that their mutilated corpses sometimes turn up in the river. Nor have they accustomed themselves to the loss of those who have disappeared and have never been heard from again. The Vicaria de la Solidaridad, an organization of the Catholic Church that is acting as a center for information, meetings, and aid, can take a great deal of credit for seeing to it that no one accepts such losses as normal. One of the overworked women there quipped to me: "We're on a hunger strike, too. I haven't had time to eat for days." The Vicaria should get the Nobel Prize for Peace, not only for what it has done but also as encouragement for all countries threatened by fascism.

For my young comrades

One plus a friend plus a friend plus a friend
don't say that makes four
the whole is greater than the sum of its parts
small numbers mean friendship
large ones revolution

Begin with what you can count on your fingers
for a friend does not dominate
a friend always has time
or knows someone else who does
a friend always finds an answer
or knows someone else who will
a friend is always competent
or will find someone else who is

Small numbers provide a network
large ones build the new city

A panel discussion on the holy spirit

It is present in silence someone says
taking twenty minutes to say it
it is present in friendship
another reads from her paper never once looking up
an old woman tells of the times in her life
when she felt the spirit move

I am too sad to speak
in el salvador I begin
people are being put to death
one way or another
put to death without exception
sometimes it's merely called exile
often it's torture
preceding the murder
and always people are killed
silenced for good
one way or another

Holy spirit
you can be killed
they can exile you
and make you disappear
you are not with us
while I'm spelling this out
as precisely as I can with my exhausted voice
the spiritless void engulfs me
the absence swallows me up
no I say once more to this void
no I say to what is here
no I say and thus repeat
veni creator spiritus
in this spiritless time

Christ in El Salvador

Mass murders in El Salvador continue. In the logic of imperialism, which cannot afford "to lose El Salvador now that Nicaragua has been lost," the resistance of the people to government terror calls for a vietnamization of this country too: the dislocation of the population, saturation bombing, eradication of the opposition, terrorism against anyone who dares even to mention the names of those who have been killed.

All this is happening in a Catholic country in which the majority of Christians have sided with the people and with the struggle for the people's rights. Churches are no longer places of ceremonial sacredness that are spared or avoided by combatants. They are again becoming places where the people assemble and where the struggle takes place. There, at the same time that the gospel is read aloud, the names of the missing are read aloud too.

In the cathedrals, the persecuted seek asylum. The churches are sanctuaries where the police and the military have no authority. Along with strikes, occupations of churches are the most important means of resistance that noncombatants have. The result is that more and more acts of violence are taking place in cathedrals. Murder in the cathedral is no longer an unusual occurrence. The bomb attack while the murdered opposition leaders were lying in state demonstrates this clearly. The terrorist organizations have announced they will continue "to hunt down communists, among whom we include Jesuits and other Christomarxist priests."

Why is the church in El Salvador being persecuted? Oscar Romero, archbishop of San Salvador, wrote a few months before he was murdered: "We have to be the church of the poor and serve them as loyally as we are obliged to serve Christ. And the first thing we must do is make them conscious of their own dignity so that they, through that same Christ, can some day profit from true liberation." The dignity of the oppressed is the object of the struggle, teaching them not to let themselves be pushed around.

Public relations

For the year 1980
the pentagon earmarked twenty-eight million dollars
for public relations

Given the magnitude of the task
that is a minuscule sum
two hundred million people live in the united states
each one of them must be kept
from thinking
each one of them must learn
not to use his or her eyes
and to suppress the old instincts
giving a glass of water to someone dying of thirst
giving a parcel of land to someone starving to death
still comes natural to many
even the need to use one's intelligence
is hard to eradicate
given the magnitude of the task
twenty-eight million dollars
for brainwashing
is amazingly little

The church is being persecuted because it is taking an increasingly strong stand on the side of the people. It is not being prevented from performing certain cultic ceremonies. The interference is aimed against its proclamation of the gospel, of the message that God has taken sides with the poor. In El Salvador, what used to be an organization devoted to the perpetuation of religious custom has become more and more the church of Jesus Christ, a church that takes part in the resistance.

It is Christ who is being tortured in El Salvador. His friends are the ones who are being abducted. It is his house that is being bombed.

Imagine for a moment that bloody persecutions of these proportions were taking place in an Eastern bloc country. The bourgeois press would experience a fit of piety. Its writers would be outraged in the depths of their souls. The house of God would be pronounced "sacred"; the persecuted priests would be "martyrs"; the persecutors would be called the Antichrist. None of this happens in the case of El Salvador, because the object of the struggle here is not the privileges of the church. The object here is the dignity of the poor.

The official propaganda of the government in El Salvador claims that these battles between the people and their murderers are "clashes between groups from the extreme right and left." The military and the government are supposedly "standing in the middle" and trying to create law and order. This is the very role that the church is expected to fill in El Salvador, and it is the one propagated by the church in West Germany.

When Cardinal Höffner was asked to express solidarity with the Christians in El Salvador, he made the statement that his "inquiries as to whether large numbers of Catholics had been killed during religious services led to the conclusion that these rumors could not be substantiated." How, indeed, could they be substantiated in a country living under a reign of brutal terror?

The result is that the appropriate response to the martyrdom of these people never comes. There is no outcry from the civilized world, no prayer said for the victims (although heaven was deluged with prayers for the American hostages in Iran). There is no protest against this genocide, no statement of solidarity with the oppressed. The pope managed to travel to Latin America in 1979 without making any mention whatsoever of the priests and nuns, the workers and young people who have been tortured to death.

Roger Vekemans, S.J., Latin America's leading anticommunist, was shameless enough to give a new definition to the word "martyrdom"—not one that looks to the faithful and their understanding of their faith but one that takes the torturers as its point of departure. Vekemans makes a distinction between victims who were killed by non-Christians and those killed by Christians. Christian killers were motivated only by "human malice," whereas religious hatred and a satanic system accounted for the crimes of non-Christian killers (*Publik-Forum,* vol. 17, 1980, p. 9). The dead are thus deprived even of their deaths, and those who give their lives are deprived of the sincerity of their devotion. We cannot remind ourselves of this point too often: there is a church of the powerful and a church of the poor. They can be distinguished by the alliances they form.

The mass murders continue in El Salvador. It is not Christian arrogance that moves us to say that it is Christ who is being tortured in El Salvador. That is a simple expression of faith. Just as he was called a "blasphemer" because he had broken with the god of the ruling classes, so he is called a "communist" today because he has broken with the god of international capitalism. The spiritual side of this struggle is not a peripheral aspect of it (and to say it was would be to speak from the arrogance of Western European Enlightenment). This struggle for liberation draws its very life from the spirit of the Jewish prophets and of Jesus' partisanship for those deprived of their rights.

I have no political analysis of resistance to offer that justifies hope. We have to expect the worst, for a while. But I know from the tradition that sustains the struggling and suffering people of El Salvador that terror will not have the last word. Death does not mean the end of everything. He could not be killed.

> It would suit the rulers of this world just fine
> if there were justice only after death,
> if only then the tyranny of tyrants,
> if only then the slavery of slaves,
> would be forgotten [Kurt Marti, "Easter Song"].

Or, to use the resurrectional invocation that Latin American freedom fighters use when thousands of voices call out together *"¡presente!"*: Victor Jara, *¡presente!* Salvador Allende, *¡presente!* Oscar Romero, *¡presente!* Juan Chacón, 23-year-old secretary general of the Revolutionary People's Bloc, *¡presente!* And many thousands more, *¡presente!*

The lord of history

And in fifteen hundred and twenty-five
in the peasants' war in germany
a rainbow rose
the earth shall not be cursed

And in nineteen eighty
in the war in el salvador
the guerrillas are celebrating mass
the dead shall not have suffered torture in vain

And in fifteen hundred and twenty-five
the peasants trusted god
who had allied himself with the earth
and they set out with pitchforks

And in nineteen eighty
the *campesinos* believe in the maiden maria
the mighty he will cast from their thrones
they sing the old song

And in fifteen hundred and twenty-five
god betrayed the peasants
and he once again cursed
the earth that knows not mine and thine

And in nineteen eighty
god made a deal with the rich
you see them grinning humbly on tv
they know they're on the side of the lord of history

To know that
    and still refuse
    to believe in tanks and stocks and bonds
to know that
    and not end up deranged
    like friedrich h* in his tower on the neckar
to know that
    and still pray
    in the name of the tortured

*Friedrich Hölderlin (1770–1843), eminent lyric poet, suffered from serious mental illness for the last forty years of his life and occupied a tower room overlooking the Neckar River in Tübingen from 1806 until his death.

Polack organization or materialistic spirituality

The strikes krystof tells us were planned
the many small underground papers
the meetings where you can see who is speaking
what the politbureau spouts isn't language at all
most of them rumor had it were in favor of using force
but the spokesman for the secret police
argued against bringing in the military and dogs and tear gas

I don't know krystof says where the capital of poland is
in krakow where the kings used to be crowned
lech walesa stood there too
and the strike leaders in the market square swore solemnly
to die for freedom if it should come to that
but perhaps krystof smiles the capital of poland
is in czestochowa where the madonna is

They can undo this only with much bloodshed
and tears I believe in angels you know krystof says
I can see our guardian angel spread out his wings
and krystof spreads out his arms as he talks
and smiles his mystical mathematical smile
the spirit is around us he says
and those who were shot ten years ago
are here the strike is a monument to them

And when he said that the room became warm
and bright with the many dead

Christ is dying in washington

Just as we were leaving
to speak out against the arms buildup
with a few thousand people in front of the white house
the loudspeakers at the station announced
that one hundred thousand people were coming to town
to save washington for christ
to protect children from homosexual teachers
and to keep young women from being in charge
of their own lives

We were only seventeen thousand
no loudspeaker took notice of us
we wanted to talk about the children in the ghettos
where so many teachers are being fired
where the schools function like prisons
we wanted to talk about the kids who end up in jail
or in the army
and about the jobs
a peaceful economy creates
there weren't many of us and the rain came down in torrents
the whole way

We have to stop the decline in morals
one of their leaders said
and the decline of the military

On the way home
a fellow demonstrator said to me
don't let it get to you washington will not be for christ
even if they buy up more radio stations
and teach people to hate themselves and others

But christ I said to him
is dying right here in washington

Amerindians: Museum Pieces
and Third-class Citizens

Excerpts from an Interview with
Two Priests of the "Guatemalan Church in Exile"
in Und sie fordern nur das Land und ihr Leben
(Munich: Informationsstelle Guatemala, 1980).

Document

Like other Amerindian peoples, the Indians of Guatemala have a history with great traditions, with high cultural and social values, and with great possibilities for growth. The Indians make up the majority of the population in Guatemala, and ever since the conquest they have been dominated, enslaved, and oppressed. Although they have been dominated all this time, they have not been defeated.

For over four hundred and fifty years the Guatemalan Indians have been embroiled in a horrible struggle for survival, and they have survived in spite of massacres too numerous to count, in spite of humiliation and total exploitation. They keep on fighting to show that they are a great people, full of dignity and genuine humanity.

Even in Guatemala, where racism between whites and Indians is taken for granted, whites are beginning to see Indians as human beings, to respect them, to see them as people with the same potential value as whites. Efforts are being made to "raise them to the level of whites." But is that really progress? In many ways, the Indians have achieved a higher order of humanity and social behavior.

Wisdom of the indians

Every day
to touch the earth with your feet
to warm yourself at the fire
to plunge into the water
to let the air caress you

To know that a day without those four
sister water brother fire
mother earth father sky
is a lost day

A day in the war
we are waging
against everything

Our brand of civilization has deprived us of many of the values the Indians still retain. Our civilization is nothing but a consumer society, egotistical, without regard for others, a civilization that lives at the expense of others. It is a civilization of clocks, machines, and weapons that rule us; we do not rule them. The Indians, however, have preserved values that may help us someday to lead different, more conscious, and more humane lives.

I lived in an Indian community in which everyone had the right to come and say, "I need this or that piece of land to sow seed on and cultivate." And everyone got as much as they asked for. This reflects the Indian sense of community. They never ask for land to own privately, as their personal property, but as land that they cultivate as part of the community. I visited many Indian communities that have been fighting for communal lands for over eighty years. The word "communal" holds great meaning for the Indian population; the feeling for the life of the community is a profound and fundamental thing in every Indian. This is also true of the concept of authority. For the Indians someone in authority is not a chief or dictator who assumes leadership. There is always someone who acts as spokesman for the community, but these authorities or leaders can easily be replaced if the community feels they no longer reflect what it wants.

The community appoints its own leaders. Leaders cannot come to power themselves by force of their own will or by virtue of certain capabilities they have. The strength of the Indian sense of identity is demonstrated by the fact that the first thing Guatemalan military authorities do with Indians they have conscripted by force is to strip them of their values and their Indian identity. The soldiers do this by taking the Indians to brothels. This is a totally unfamiliar and alien experience for them because prostitution is unknown in the Indian culture. We know that the Indians marry very early and that a man can have several women. But there is only one woman who is his wife. The respect that the family has for the wife is very great.

There are no orphans in Indian society. There are, of course, children whose parents have died, but the Indians never speak of these children as orphans or treat them as orphans. These children belong to the community, which reacts like a family and immediately takes such children in. Human relationships are valued highly in Indian social life.

On holidays such as New Year's Day children and adults exchange small gifts—a cup of cocoa or coffee, for example. This is an expression of a highly developed capacity for communication within the families. With these small gifts, the Indians show their special respect for the older members of their community.

In our civilization, those who are no longer in the production process are, by contrast, of no use anymore. They are stuck in a home for the elderly because they are no longer of value and should not be allowed to get in the way. The principle is: you are what you can do. That would be unthinkable for the Indians. They have immense respect for the elderly in their communities.

I have no specialized knowledge in the sphere of Indian studies. I am just telling you what I saw and experienced. And perhaps I have not had time enough to grasp and convey all this in more intellectual terms. But there is one thing I can say: all these values of Indian culture are important. They can serve as models for us, inspiring us to make our society more humane.

Speaking Out for the Silenced

Epilogue to Und sie fordern nur das Land und ihr
Leben, *cf. pp. 154–57 above*

I want to try to say why this document from Guatemala affects
me the way it does; I shall single out only one detail to convey what
it is that disturbs me so deeply: the first thing that is done with
young Indians forced into military service is to take them to a
brothel. Military training begins with the eradication of cultural
identity.

That is not, by the way, a purely exotic practice or one limited to
Latin American countries. Alcoholism and the existence of brothels
are as much a part of the capitalist system as driving people off
their land or driving them into exile. I can imagine the reactions of
a young Indian having his first experience of army terror ("Made in
Israel," for example). Perhaps he will become mute like his brother
in North America in *One Flew over the Cuckoo's Nest*. Perhaps he
will learn to fight.

From this one detail, it became clear to me how oppression
functions.

• Indians are being robbed of their land and of the treasures it
contains. They are members of an "inferior race." They have not
yet achieved the technological level of the ruling class. Their
traditional economy and their communal life function differently.
Either they have to be forced to adjust to the culture of the brothel,
or they have to be eliminated. White rulers know of only two
possible ways of dealing with members of "inferior" racial
groupings: subjugation or liquidation. Either into the brothel with
them, the factory, the army, the ghetto, the reservation—or into
machine-gun fire, forced sterilization, saturation bombing. A

The tower of babel

Sure we're working day and night
we use floodlights on the night shift
we're moving ahead on schedule
you can bet your life on it

We're making bricks faster now
whether fathers have time to see their kids
doesn't matter we keep to
the highest standard here

Of course the tower has nothing but apartments in it
there's no call for anything else
people only sleep here anyway
what are you talking about

And when it got colder
we turned up the thermostat
and when misunderstandings began to crop up
we ordered more alcohol
and when people started hearing strange languages
we said just keep on working and consuming
this spoken communication business
will take care of itself

system that forces onto members of another race the alternative of being enslaved or being murdered we call *racism*.

• The oppression of half of humanity—the female half—has to be deliberately taught and carried out. The bestiality that the military pursues on behalf of or with the tacit approval of major international concerns is designed to make women into objects that can be used, destroyed, and discarded. A system that harms, oppresses, and destroys people on the basis of their sex we call *sexism*.

•The rich wage this dirty war against the poor, who are to be kept silent and stripped of all their rights. Any attempt that people make to organize themselves in any way that deviates from this dependent status is brutally crushed. It is a crime to form a co-op in the villages. The land is not there to be cultivated but to be owned and exploited. The ruling power elite in the country—that small class that supports the government—tries to win its share of the profits of multinational corporations. This combination of neoliberal economic policy à la Milton Friedman and an international division of labor as planned by the Trilateral Commission results in the exiling or eradication of the original inhabitants. Experience has shown that this policy works best when the national power elite—the military and the police—take part in it. This system we call international *capitalism*.

Racism, sexism, and capitalism blend together into a unity. It is illusory to think that a peaceful route to capitalism can be found, one that does not make any use of capitalism's two bloody allies. The young Indian who is forced into the military, sent to a brothel, and then trained to kill his compatriots is an example of how oppression functions. Perhaps he will turn around and aim his rifle in the opposite direction. There are many hopeful signs that this kind of resistance is taking shape.

What is the attitude of Christian churches to these forms of oppression? The interview (above) with two priests speaks for itself. Everything they say reveals that they have broken with racism, sexism, and international capitalism. They have taken their stand on the side of the people, and like thousands of others who have worked for the people, they were interrogated and deported. They ran the risk of torture and death.

Esthetic and existential experience

A good story
a true film
a useful dream
    these are houses to live in
    you help wash the dishes in the kitchen
    you put on the clothes you find lying around
    you join in the laughter
    you join in the screaming
    when you've been at home
    with everything long enough and without fear
    then you'll become
the teller of a true story
the director of a useful film
the I that dreams a good dream
    when you've relinquished all distance
    and have lost yourself in everyone
    you'll go back and start yourself
to tell what will help
to film those who fight
to dream what will move you forward
    the changing world will then be
    what it was in the beginning
behold everything was beautiful

In recent years, word has spread even in the Federal Republic that class struggle cannot be put aside when we pass through the portals of a church. The churches do not represent the interests of only one class. The role of the church as an institution is not comparable to that of the police. More and more Christians, by reason of their faith, are casting their lot with the people and against those who rule over them; with the poor and against those who grow rich from the poverty of others; with the people's struggle and against those who witness torture and terror and say nothing. Theological decisions like Christ's decision to side with the poor without reservation and without any meaningless blather about peace that tries to gloss over class differences—theological decisions like that are always political decisions too. In the United States, millions of people who had never dreamed of praying for the victims of the shah of Iran's torturers prayed for the American hostages in Iran.

Whether I portray Christ as a judge wearing the symbols of Roman power or as a revolutionary wearing the symbols of a despised criminal is not a matter of theological hairsplitting. Portraying him as a revolutionary gives cultural expression to the suffering and struggle of human beings. Whether the church building is an asylum for the homeless, for "protesters against death," as the pastor and socialist Blumhardt has called Christians, an asylum for the persecuted, or whether it is a hall reserved for the coronations of heads of state—those are questions that are being fought out today.

We cannot remind ourselves too often that there is a church of the powerful and a church of the poor. They can be distinguished by the number of their adherents, and among the adherents of the church of the poor are the dead, with whom Christians feel a strong bond. Anyone who reads the interview with the two priests from Guatemala will sense this link with those who have been murdered. These two men are not speaking just for themselves; they are one with the people on whose behalf they raise their voices. And "the people" in the mystico-political sense in which the word is used in Latin American liberation struggles always includes the people's dead.

It is in the interest of the church of the powerful to deny that two churches exist, one for the oppressed, another for the oppressors. Official propaganda in Guatemala claims that the battles between the people and the murderers of the people are "conflicts between groups of the extreme right and left." The military and the government, the propagandists claim, stand "in the middle" and are trying to restore law and order. This argument is widely accepted in church circles too. American Protestant missionaries do not see Christ in oppressed *Indios* and in raped and murdered women but as standing "above" all this, somewhere beyond the suffering and struggle of the people. That is why the ruling classes promote and reward this kind of piety. The church of the powerful is well versed in this kind of hypocrisy.

I am all too familiar with these tactics from Europe and from the Federal Republic of Germany, where the church of the powerful always bends over backwards to say both no and yes, at the same time. It says "nyes" to racism, "nyes" to sexism, "nyes" to capitalism. If you want to avoid solidarity, if you want to preach the Christ of the mighty on earth now and in heaven later, then it is wise to adopt these strategies:

• Disregard an interview such as the one with the two priests.

• Examine its "validity" from as many perspectives as possible.

• Insist that other subjects—for example the threat of modern society to the Christian family—are more important.

By now, with the murder of Archbishop Oscar Romero, it has become clear that this "nyes," this false neutrality, amounts to complicity in crime. What is the German Bishops' Conference waiting for? What is the Synod of the Protestant Church in Germany waiting for? What further reports do we have to hear before we open our mouths and speak a clear and audible no to the racists, the sexists, the capitalists, and to all who profit from these practices? There is, of course, little point in expecting something from "the church" as long as we do not practice solidarity in our own lives and so begin to be the church ourselves.

Christ made God manifest by making invisible people visible—the poor, women, all those deprived of their rights. He was, as Bonhoeffer has called him, a "human being for others." In the interview with my two brothers from Guatemala there is a statement about the church that is of great significance for us here

163

in Europe: "The church is not being persecuted because it is the church and because it practices certain religious exercises. It is being persecuted because it is trying, more or less, to side with the Indian population." And the moment it does that, it begins to be the church. It sees things through the eyes of Jesus, not of the government. It makes the invisible visible instead of leaving them in their invisibility. It speaks out for those who have been silenced, the Amerindians of Guatemala.

Ita Ford, A Nun from Brooklyn

I have been in Ronald Reagan's America for a month now, and I am trying to develop a sense of the difficulties, struggles, and suffering of the people with whom I am working, a sense of their despair over the official policy of their country, of their resistance against militarism and impoverishment. Like a foreigner who might have gone to Berlin in 1937 and seen and heard things there that were at odds with the official propaganda, who might, despite all, have caught sight of "another Germany," I too should like to convey something of "the other America," which does exist despite increasingly open displays of racism, despite the Moral Majority, which has all kinds of objections to abortion but none at all to a limited nuclear war, and despite El Salvador, the new Vietnam.

It is impossible to understand a country if we ignore its minorities. Its history remains muted if we listen only to the victors. We cannot love a country if we see only its published culture, its television culture.

I should like to sketch a portrait of an American woman, a Catholic nun, one of the four women missionaries who were murdered in El Salvador in December 1980. Ita Ford belonged to the Maryknoll Sisters, a missionary congregation of women who do not live in cloisters and wear habits but who live in slums together with the poor and are there for the poor.

Ita Ford was born in Brooklyn in 1940. At the age of 21, after graduating from college, she joined the Maryknollers. She went to Chile in 1971, just before Allende's government was toppled. The following years of hardships and persecution formed her character. In this period, her commitment to the poor grew. She learned what it meant to be a Christian who made the cause of the poor her own, to live in a *barrio* with very few personal possessions, on call day and night for people who needed a hiding place, food, clothing. In 1977 she wrote down these reflections:

Am I willing to suffer with these people here, to share the suffering of the powerless, the sense of impotence? Can I say to my neighbors: I have no solution to this situation, I have no answers, but I want to go with you, search with you. Can I seize this opportunity to evangelize myself? Can I see and accept my own poverty as I see other poor people doing?

Perhaps someday the notes and letters of this nun and of Maura Clark, her sister in Maryknoll, will be read among Christians the way we read the letters and journals of Dietrich Bonhoeffer today. To be a martyr means to be a witness, a witness of truth, a witness of love, a witness of resistance and of voluntary devotion to others. Ita Ford could have had a different life, as could Bonhoeffer, who passed up the chance for a brilliant academic career when he chose to return to Nazi Germany.

In August 1979 Ita wrote a birthday letter to her sixteen-year-old niece Jennifer. I want to quote from this letter, which another Maryknoll sister gave to me, to convey something of the spirit that sustains people like Ita and Maura and Dorothy and Jean. Ita wrote to Jennifer:

> Most important of all I love you and wonder how you are. But you know that, and you can count on it whether you're an angel or a brat, a genius or a dope. In the end, much will depend on you yourself and on what you decide to do with your life.
>
> Much of what I want to tell you is not just the thing for a jolly birthday chat, but it is real. Yesterday I was looking down on a sixteen-year-old who had just been killed a few hours before. I know of a lot of children, some younger than this one, who are dead. This is a horrible time for young people in El Salvador. So much idealism and commitment is being destroyed.
>
> The reasons for why so many people have been killed are somewhat complicated, but there are a few clear and simple ones. One is that many people have found meaning in their lives—they make sacrifices, fight, even die. And whether they live to be sixteen or sixty or ninety, they know what they are living for. In many ways they're lucky.

Brooklyn is not El Salvador. But a few things remain true wherever you are. And no matter how old you are. What I want to say is that I hope you'll succeed in finding what will give life a deep meaning for you. Something that's worth living for, perhaps even worth dying for, something that gives you strength and inspires you and makes you able to go on.

I can't tell you what that might be. You have to find and choose and love it yourself. All I can do is encourage you to keep an eye out for it and support you in your search.

Ita Ford had learned the lessons of the poor in Chile. When Archbishop Oscar Romero in San Salvador called for help, she was willing to go. When she arrived, Romero had just been murdered. The new beginning was not easy for her. She missed her sisters in the congregation and her friends. It was not easy to win the confidence of people who, terrorized by the political situation, were living in constant fear. She worked in an emergency relief program for refugees. She wrote:

I don't know whether it's in spite of or because of all the horror, the fear, the confusion, and lawlessness—but I know that it is right to be here. I think that we are here in and for El Salvador now, that the answers to the questions will come when we need them, that someday we will go together with the Salvadorans in faith, on the same road that is full of obstacles and detours and sometimes washed out.

Ita and her fellow nuns felt responsible to relieve the suffering of the wounded, the homeless, and the hungry. They realized what the political implications were of feeding the hungry in a country torn by an undeclared civil war. There were rumors that they were on the hit list of several right-wing terrorist organizations.

At the end of November, Ita took part in a five-day conference in Nicaragua. Those days must have been, as her sisters report, a time of profound healing for her. At the start of her work in El Salvador, she had lost her best friend in an accident. At the final worship service, she read a passage from one of Oscar Romero's last sermons. It was a prophesy that came to pass for her only twenty-four hours later:

167

Christ asks us not to fear persecution, because—believe me, brothers and sisters—whoever has cast his or her lot with the poor will have to endure the same fate as the poor, and in El Salvador we know what the fate of the poor is: to disappear, to be tortured, to be a prisoner, to be found dead.

The sign of political hope that has followed on the death of these four women is the growing opposition of the American Catholic Church, the opposition of its bishops' conference, to the political and military interference of the United States in El Salvador.

In mid-January about fifteen hundred people took part in a worship service in front of the White House in Washington. It was a memorial service "for the four and the ten thousand" who were murdered in El Salvador in 1979. Four white coffins were carried to the Capitol, along with a large symbolic coffin for the children, young people, *campesinos,* and women, for all those, primarily noncombatants, who were murdered on suspicion of "subversion" and "terrorism." How much longer will this repetition of Vietnam's history continue?

Beyond political hope, there is a spiritual hope that sustains people like Ita Ford. As the Bible says: "This has taught us love—that he gave up his life for us; and we, too, ought to give up our lives for our brothers" (1 John 3:16).

On December 2, 1980, Ita Ford and her three companions did just that.

A story from the talmud and questions for us

When god had created heaven and earth
he loved both equally
the heavens rejoiced
and praised god's glory
but the earth wept
    did you hear the earth weep
    did you forget the dying fish
    was the old tree in your way
    did you miss the birds
    did you hear the earth weep
the earth gave three reasons for weeping
you keep me she said at a distance
but the heavens are close to you
and rejoice in your glory
    did you come to comfort the earth when she was ravaged
    did you join with the pack and reckon the booty
    did you see the beauty of her old face with all its crevices
    did you show everyone how god's closeness makes her shine
    did you come to comfort the earth
my nourishment said the earth
you've given over to the heavens
and the heavens are fed from your own table
    did you hear the earth's complaints
    to get rid of the lords above who wouldn't like that
    or to sit at a table with plenty for all
    did you forget that she can feed everyone
    did you hear the earth's complaints against the lords
whatever lives on me the earth said
is doomed to death
death that does not enter the realms of heaven
why then said the earth should I not weep
    did you hear the earth speak
    did you understand the language of the earth
    did you listen to the lies of the heavenly immortals

did you share the earth's sadness
did you hear the earth speak
according to the books god comforted the earth
but he didn't promise her closeness
better food or life free of death
don't be downhearted earth
someday you too he said
will be among those who rejoice
did you ever see god give comfort
except through you or me
did you rejoice with the earth
did you learn from her to rejoice
did you see god give comfort
were you a comfort for the earth

Alternative tv

The old man on the screen sang
in a loud and shaky voice
and had probably never been very clean
in addition he had hardly any teeth left
a miner with black lung
of course he spoke dialect and his grammar was bad
why after all should he
show his best side to the camera

When god turns on his tv
he sees old people like that
they sing
in a loud and shaky voice
and the camera of the holy spirit
shows the dignity of these people
and makes god say
that is very beautiful

Later
when we have abolished tv as it exists
and are allowed to look at the skin of aging women
and are unafraid of eyes
that have lost their lashes in weeping
when we respect work
and the workers have become visible
and sing
in a loud and shaky voice

Then we shall see
real people
and be happy about it
like god

Make love not war

On the Occasion of the Pope's Visit to Germany

The pope talks about birth control
he doesn't talk about nuclear weapons

Christ speaks about the birds of the air
and the lilies of the field

They arm themselves not
neither do they practice killing
nor hide in tanks

Just as a man and a woman
make love
put aside more and more weapons
become vulnerable
and happy

Of related interest . . .

Dorothee Sölle
REVOLUTIONARY PATIENCE

"*Revolutionary Patience* is an intriguing title. It speaks to the existential situation of many of us on the left in America today. In this slender book of poems Sölle shows her solidarity with the poor and the oppressed and her identification of the heritage of Jesus with their cause. The poems are reflective, not strident. They are not propaganda. There is a sadness in these poems, a sense of the tentative, of sacrifice without guarantees, but washed clean of self-pity and sentimentality by the discipline of concrete work and hope. *Revolutionary Patience* gives voice to a seasoned radicalism, one that is ready to stay the distance. It is helpful reading for those who find they cannot give up the tasks of fundamental change, nor avoid its pain."

Religious Studies Review

"Dr. Sölle has taught philosophy, literature, and theology at several German universities. Her works on *Christ, the Representative, Political Theology*, and *Suffering* have already been translated into English. This is a series of prayer-poems which attempt to 'make sense, in the light of the Gospel, of a world brutally scarred by oppression, filled with the cries of the hungry and the hunted.' "

Theology Digest

"Her poetry and prayers on the experience of suffering 'sting their way into the reader's mind and heart.' "

Response

ISBN 0-88344-439-9 *88pp. Paper $3.95*

Adolfo Pérez Esquivel
(Winner of the 1980 Nobel Peace Prize)
CHRIST IN A PONCHO
Witnesses to the Non-Violent Struggle in Latin America

The Nobel Prize, says Pérez Esquivel, reaches far beyond his simple person, going to all his brothers and sisters in Latin America—especially to the poorest and the most oppressed, and to the hundreds and thousands of nameless women and men who are battling for the dignity of the humble and fighting for respect for the ones they call the "marginalized"—the little people whom economic growth has passed right by: peasants robbed of their land; Indians scorned by modern society; the forgotten inhabitants of sprawling suburbs or shantytowns; Bolivian miners' wives; workers fired in São Paulo or Mexico city because they dared to strike; and the mothers of the fifteen thousand young people "missing" in Argentina today. It is a whole Latin America in anguish and agony. But it is a Latin America full of hope, too, and already winning victories.

"*Christ in a Poncho* offers an invaluable introduction to nonviolence in Latin America. The biographical sketch of Adolfo Pérez Esquivel, his own splendid 'ant and elephant' essay, and the very concrete case histories portray and underscore the urgency and difficulty of the nonviolent witness in that beleaguered region 'where tomorrow struggles to be born.' Orbis has rendered a signal service in making this unique book available."

Richard A. Chartier, Fellowship

ISBN 0-88344-104-7   *144pp. Paper $6.95*

Dom Helder Camara
THE DESERT IS FERTILE (2nd Printing)

"Camara's brief essays and poems are arresting for their simplicity and depth of vision, and are encouraging because of the realistic yet quietly hopeful tone with which they argue for sustained action toward global justice."   *Commonweal*

ISBN 0-88344-093-8   *illustrated, 75pp. Paper $4.95*

John J. Ansbro
MARTIN LUTHER KING, JR.
The Making of a Mind

"John Ansbro has traced the roots and the development of the inner man—King—and his quest for truth and his experiment in the conquest of violence. This is a unique contribution. For those who wish to know the inner King and the concepts that underlay his committment to nonviolence, human rights, and peace, this book is a must."
Bayard Rustin, President,
A. Philip Randolph Educational Fund

"Professor Ansbro has written a first-rate guide that is a 'must' for future scholars interested in the intellectual and spiritual formation of Martin Luther King."
Rev. William Sloane Coffin, Jr.,
Senior Minister, The Riverside Church, New York City

"This is a truly remarkable study of the development of Dr. King's belief in the theory of nonviolent action in the quest for social justice. The reader, conditioned by the noble simplicity of the marches, songs, and sermons repeated in the popular portrayals of the man, is powerfully reminded that Martin Luther King, Jr., was a deeply learned and sophisticated scholar."
Ramsey Clark, former Attorney General of the U.S.

ISBN 0-88344-333-3   *368pp. Cloth $17.95*

L. John Topel
THE WAY TO PEACE (3rd Printing)
Liberation Through the Bible
*The first book in any language systematically
to trace the roots of liberation theology
in both the Old and New Testaments.*

"*The Way to Peace* is good fare. Topel traces the roots of liberation theology through the Old and New Testaments. The book is scholarly, well footnoted and fascinating reading."
Today's Parish

"The success of Topel's method results from his strict adherence to his theme and his profound understanding of the Scriptures. Theological arguments are supported by biblical references.

Excellent summaries are helpful; and notes, annotated at great length, add value to the book.''   *Spirituality Today*

"Uses the most sophisticated current scriptural tools to carve out an excellent reintroduction to the Bible and to argue that our present freedom is the World's ultimate aim.''   *America*

ISBN 0-88344-704-5   *199pp. Paper $7.95*

J. Carter Swaim
WAR, PEACE, AND THE BIBLE (2nd Printing)

A popular presentation of biblical teaching on war and peace. Especially strong on contemporary applications.

"At a time when the world is looking desperately for peace, kindness, and holiness on our beautiful, God-given planet, this book will help many Christians find a proper stand on the issues of violence, war, and armaments.''

Robert Muller, Secretary of the UN
Economic and Social Council

"I have been charmed, informed, and inspired by reading this work. I was lifted up due to the sharp, precise, fresh, and informative approach to an important contemporary problem. There is detail for the lay person and thoughtful notation and scholarly interpretation for the more advanced scholar. There is an exciting display of understanding and ability to relate to real life. The writings are a harvest of information for the person who wishes to be informed whether lay, priest-pastor, or scholar.''

Harry Brunger, National Council of the YMCA

ISBN 0-88344-752-5   *144pp. Paper $6.95*

Thomas A. Shannon
WAR OR PEACE? (2nd Printing)
The Search for New Answers

Most citizens (including their religious leaders) seem so stunned by the apocalyptic horror of what nuclear war might be that they prefer to banish the question from their minds. Yet the potential for war is constantly increasing, nations continue to stockpile weapons, and local conflagrations could burst into nuclear confrontation. We pray for peace, but know only the absence of war. Is peace possible? What is the Christian attitude toward war, on whatever scale, with whatever weapons? These questions are being raised with a new urgency, and are addressed in this supremely important book by a succession of distinguished Christians who have dedicated their lives to a search for answers. Among them, Dorothy Day, Gordon Zahn, Paul Deats, Eileen Egan, Paul Hanly Furfey, Bryan Hehir, James Finn, and Bishop Thomas Gumbleton.

"The authors both chronicle and contribute to the Roman Catholic reassessment of just-war thought, pacifism, and the relationship of church and state." *Choice*

"It's timely, useful to any thoughtful person; the writing in parts is graceful; it deserves recommendation. A couple of the essays alone would be worth the price." *Salt*

"Will likely soon be showing up on reading lists for undergraduate and seminary ethics courses." *Worldview*

ISBN 0-88344-750-9 *256pp. Paper $9.95*

Francis X. Meehan
A CONTEMPORARY SOCIAL SPIRITUALITY

Meehan, with masterful clarity, focuses the light of the Gospel and Christian ethics on the major issues troubling today's Christian: war, the draft, disarmament, economic injustice, racism, abortion, sexuality.

"Francis X. Meehan has thought long and hard about contemporary social issues. This book shows the gratifying results. It is full of insight and wisdom."

Richard A. McCormick, S.J.,
Professor of Christian Ethics, Georgetown University

ISBN 0-88344-022-9 *144pp. Paper $6.95*

Kathleen & James McGinnis
PARENTING FOR PEACE AND JUSTICE (5th Printing)

"The authors have put together their experiences as parents of three adopted children, one of whom is multiracial, and enlarged their perspective through the ideas of other parents. Believing that the family is the most important learning place, their book documents their concerns with racial equality, simple living, and nonviolence and how they and other parents have tried to counterbalance what children learn from other children and various media. What makes this book so enjoyable and useful is perhaps due to the McGinnises writing honestly of their triumphs and failures as parents on a day-to-day level. The chapters are organized around 'concerns,' beginning with teaching children about stewardship and simple living. They cover such topics as alternative celebrations and decommercializing religious holidays, recycling and appreciation of nature, spending less for clothes and snacks, and more. The McGinnises, with their free-flowing, non-reproachful style of writing, have put together an excellent resource manual for parents.'' *Friends Journal*

''An extraordinary book telling how to devise ways of teaching Christian social action in the family. The McGinnises' agenda includes stewardship/simplicity; nonviolence in the family and violence in the world; multiculturalizing family life; sex-role stereotyping; and inviting children to participate in social action. Their suggestions are practical and stimulating, well within most parents' capabilities.'' *Bulletin of the Congregational Library*

ISBN 0-88344-376-7 *154pp. Paper $4.95*

Marjorie Hope & James Young
THE STRUGGLE FOR HUMANITY
Agents of Nonviolent Change in a Violent World

''This is an immensely helpful and valuable book. The authors have rendered a very significant service in bringing together portraits of men and women who are leaders in the nonviolent struggle for social change. Hope and Young have written a book of immense importance because they have brought to it very considerable skills as writers and a deep commitment to nonviolence.'' *Occasional Bulletin of Missionary Research*

''Thoughtfully and gracefully written, and with balance, these are fascinating stories of dedicated living and a guide and inspiration to nonviolent efforts in any situation.''*Spiritual Book News*

ISBN 0-88344-468-2 · *305pp. Cloth $8.95*
ISBN 0-88344-469-0 *Paper $6.95*